T0120791

PATIENCE
PATIENCE
PATIENCE

GERALD MCDANIEL

WESTBOW
PRESS®
A DIVISION OF THOMAS NELSON
& ZONDERVAN

Copyright © 2020 Gerald McDaniel.

All rights reserved. No part of this book may be used or reproduced by
any means, graphic, electronic, or mechanical, including photocopying,
recording, taping or by any information storage retrieval system
without the written permission of the author except in the case
of brief quotations embodied in critical articles and reviews.

This book is a work of non-fiction. Unless otherwise noted, the author
and the publisher make no explicit guarantees as to the accuracy of
the information contained in this book and in some cases, names
of people and places have been altered to protect their privacy.

WestBow Press books may be ordered through booksellers or by contacting:

WestBow Press
A Division of Thomas Nelson & Zondervan
1663 Liberty Drive
Bloomington, IN 47403
www.westbowpress.com
844-714-3454

Because of the dynamic nature of the Internet, any web addresses or
links contained in this book may have changed since publication and
may no longer be valid. The views expressed in this work are solely those
of the author and do not necessarily reflect the views of the publisher,
and the publisher hereby disclaims any responsibility for them.

Any people depicted in stock imagery provided by Getty Images are models,
and such images are being used for illustrative purposes only.
Certain stock imagery © Getty Images.

Scripture taken from the King James Version of the Bible.

ISBN: 978-1-6642-0576-5 (sc)
ISBN: 978-1-6642-0577-2 (e)

Print information available on the last page.

WestBow Press rev. date: 09/28/2020

A Personal Letter to my Grandchildren

I would like to share, first of all, a partial personal testimony out of my own life. Many years ago, as a small young boy I was extremely shy and very much an introvert. I would do most anything to avoid standing up in front of people and speaking especially in front of a school class. Even in sports on the basketball court the intimidation of the crowd no matter how large or small would greatly hinder me from playing basketball as well as I was able.

I had a dear grandmother who was a precious Christian lady. When she would come to stay with our family from time to time, she would always call me her little preacher boy. I hated it because even though I was lost at the time I knew that it would mean getting up in front of people. Needless to say, I regretted it every time grandmother came around.

At the age of 20 years old I trusted Christ as my personal Savior. At the age of 21 years old, strange as it may seem, God called me to preach. My grandmother was right.

Having said this I am convinced just like grandmother was that I will have a grandchild whether born or adopted, girl or boy that God will call to take the books that I have written and learn them and be able to understand them and teach from them and use them in their ministry that God has for them.

Be advised, you will run into many that do not agree with the teachings in these books. You will probably have family that will not agree with the teachings in these books. Either way as a little girl in writing or teaching ladies or as a little boy in writing or teaching and preaching, I am convinced God will raise up one of my grandchildren to a ministry that these books will be greatly used.

Please understand at the time of this writing, there have been 4 books published and 2 written yet to be published with more to come. At this time, you may not even be born yet or adopted yet. Even though all my grandchildren are welcome to these books and will have access to these books, I am convinced as much as I am alive that God will raise up one of you with a special ministry directly related to these books.

If I live long enough, I will be able to witness this taking place, firsthand. My grandmother died before she was able to hear me preach. Please be aware that I am not writing these books as a hobby neither are they written to make money. It is a God called ministry. There will be many more books written and all my grandchildren will have access to them if that is their desire. I want to reassure you of course that I love all my grandchildren.

There will be one with a special calling. May God bless you little one and I am praying for you now even if you have not been born or adopted yet. Granddaddy loves you very much and is excited about what God will do in your life.

This letter will be published with the future books to make sure you get a copy of this letter.

Contents

1

The Plan of Salvation

Let's go through 4 H's. Honesty, Humility, Helpless, and Hope

H   #1)   *You must be HONEST enough to admit you have sinned and broken God's commands. Understand in doing so this puts you in very great danger!*

Romans 3:10 "there is none righteous, no not one."

Romans 3:23 "…all have sinned…"

I John 1:8 "if we say that we have no sin, we deceive ourselves, and the truth is not in us."

H   #2)   *You must be HUMBLE enough to admit you deserve Hell when you die.*

One sin disqualifies us from Heaven, and we have all sinned more than once.

Romans 6:23 "For the wages of sin [is] death"

Revelation 21:8 "But the fearful, and unbelieving, and the abominable, and murderers, and whoremongers, and sorcerers, and idolaters, and all liars, shall have their part in the lake which burneth with fire and brimstone: which is the second death."

H   #3)   *You must understand you are HELPLESS when it comes to you saving yourself from going to Hell when you die. There is nothing you can do to pay for your own sin.*

Ephesians 2:8-9 For by grace are ye saved through faith; and that not of yourselves: it is the gift of God: not of works, lest any man should boast.

Titus 3:5 Not by works of righteousness which we have done, but according to his mercy he saved us, by the washing of regeneration, and renewing of the Holy Ghost;

Galatians 2:16 Knowing that a man is not justified by the works of the law, but by the faith of Jesus Christ, even we have believed in Jesus Christ, that we might be justified by the faith of Christ, and not by the works of the law: for by the works of the law shall no flesh be justified.

Understand when I say HELPLESS it means you cannot surrender your life to Christ for salvation. You have no life to surrender. You are dead in trespasses and sins. You cannot yet make Jesus the Lord of your life because you have no life.

Jesus will not be Lord of your life until He is Savior of your soul. You cannot turn from your sins because you are dead in your sins. You must see yourself HELPLESS at the Mercy of God. Now you are ready for H # 4.

H   #4)   *You are helpless but not hopeless. Your HOPE must be in Jesus, God's Son and what he has done for you on the cross when He died there. Jesus is the only one that paid for your sins when he died on the cross. He was buried and arose again. You must ask Jesus to be your personal Savior and ask Jesus to save you from Hell. If you are depending on church membership to save you, that means you are not depending on Jesus to save you. If you are depending on the good deeds you do to save you, that means you are not depending on Jesus to save you. If you are depending on baptism to save you, that means you are not depending on Jesus to save you. It must be Jesus and what Jesus did for you on the cross that you are depending on to save you. Nothing else can go with this. Jesus is the only one who paid for your sins on the cross so Jesus is the only one who can save you.*

Romans 5:8 But God commendeth his love toward us, in that, while we were yet sinners, Christ died for us.

I Peter 3:18 For Christ also hath once suffered for sins, the just for the unjust, that he might bring us to God, being put to death in the flesh but quickened by the Spirit.

Hebrews 10:12 But this man (JESUS) after he hath offered one sacrifice for sins for ever, sat down on the right hand of God.

John 14:6 Jesus saith unto him, I am the way, the truth, and the life: no man cometh unto the Father, but by me.

Acts 4:12 Neither is there salvation in any other: for there is none other name under heaven given among men, whereby we must be saved.

John 3:16 For God so loved the world, that he gave his only begotten Son, that whosoever believeth in him should not perish, but have everlasting life.

Ask Jesus to save you before it is too late:

Romans 10:13 For whosoever shall call upon the name of the Lord shall be saved.

2

Opening Comments

This author is aware of the tremendous daring act it is to write a book on "Patience." Trust me. It is not easy to preach on patience, let alone to write a whole book on that subject.

In my personal life I have always been the type of person that was early for everything and in a hurry for everything. For whatever reason I had a very strong dislike for being late for anything. If I knew something was coming to me, I was anxious to get it or get it over with whether it was good or bad. As a child it could have been a birthday present or a Christmas present or even a spanking. It did not matter. I would, if possible, cut corners and make short cuts for anything that was in my life to save time and get things over with and done even if they were bad. Part of the side-effects that were produced in me due to this over-anxious lifestyle through the years was that it made me a very impatient type of a person. I even combined my Senior year of high school with my first year of Technical College just to get them both out of the way. I have always had a real problem with waiting on things. Even my engagement to be married was less than 6 months long. I knew that it was God's will, so I thought, why wait? For what it is worth, I also was even actually born 2 months pre-mature. Now, I am faced with the task of writing a book on what the Bible says about patience. You can imagine the amount of crow I am eating while writing this book.

The reader might think that it is also interesting that during the time that God has led me to write this book, the Corona Virus is sweeping across the United States and the world. You may know first-hand how much patience is needed to get through the times of this virus successfully.

Also, during the time of writing this book, I am dealing with a severe case of gout in my right hand and yes, I am right-handed.

With that being said, as usual, we will go to the Bible and see what God has to say about patience. It will not take long to find out that God is very big on patience. God sees patience as a necessary element in the character of every believer and in every phase of the believer's life in order for that believer to be spiritually successful. For an example, notice the following passage.

(Luke 21:19) In your patience possess ye your souls.

Your life and the stability of your own soul is depending on your patience. The passage above speaks volumes for telling us how important patience should be in every believer's life. By the way, Luke 21:19 is a direct quote from Christ.

Now, notice another passage concerning patience versus humanity.

(1Thess 5:14) Now we exhort you, brethren, warn them that are unruly, comfort the feebleminded, support the weak, be patient toward all men.

We must warn and comfort and support humanity with patience. We must be patient with the unruly, the feebleminded, and the weak. When God commands us to be patient toward all men, of course, that "all" means "all." This includes unbelievers, believers, young and old, rich and poor, and even to be patient with our self. Please read Chapter 10 of this Book for more details on patience toward humanity.

It is also true that impatience can get between the believer and receiving some of the promises of God. Please see Chapter 16 in this Book for more details on patience versus promises. In other words, impatience can hinder us or even delay us from receiving some of the promises that God gives us. I say some because one of the promises that is instant is eternal life the very moment you trust Christ as your Savior. Notice the following passages.

(1John 2:25) And <u>this is the promise that he hath promised us, *even* eternal life</u>.

(1John 5:13) <u>These things have I written unto you that believe on the name of the Son of God; that ye may know that ye have eternal life</u>, and that ye may believe on the name of the Son of God.

(John 5:24) Verily, verily, I say unto you, <u>He that heareth my word, and believeth on him that sent me, hath everlasting life, and shall not come into condemnation</u>; but is passed from death unto life.

(John 3:16) <u>For God so loved the world, that he gave his only begotten Son, that whosoever believeth in him should not perish, but have everlasting life.</u>

(John 3:18) <u>He that believeth on him is not condemned</u>: but he that believeth not is condemned already, because he hath not believed in the name of the only begotten Son of God.

(John 3:36) <u>He that believeth on the Son hath everlasting life: and he that believeth not the Son shall not see life; but the wrath of God abideth on him.</u>

We need to be aware of the importance and power of patience in our spiritual lives as believers, and how our patience relates to the promises of God. Notice the verses below.

(Heb 6:12) That ye be not slothful, but followers of them who <u>through faith and patience inherit the promises.</u>

(Heb 6:15) And so, <u>after he had patiently endured, he obtained the promise</u>.

(Heb 10:36) For <u>ye have need of patience, that, after ye have done the will of God, ye might receive the promise.</u>

Finally, when we are trying to live right and do right and things still seem to go wrong, impatience raises its ugly head again. We seem to suffer in spite of doing right. Notice the following passage.

(1Pet 2:20) For what glory *is it*, if, when ye be buffeted for your faults, ye shall take it patiently? but if, <u>when ye do well, and suffer *for it*, ye take it patiently, this *is* acceptable with God.</u>

For a quick summary, the individual with patience will not jump to conclusions and will not over-react and will not be guilty of guessing at decisions. The individual with patience carefully listens to others. The individual with patience will not panic or get ahead of God but will safely trust in God. The individual with patience is stable in his or her ways and will not quit on God. The individual with patience will endure whatever test or trial God has for him and will keep learning and growing for the rest of his life. <u>The individual with patience has a huge advantage over the rest of the impatient world.</u>

With being as thorough as I can, this author will do his best to show from the Bible what God has to say about "PATIENCE." Hopefully, the reader will have enough patience to read and study this whole book.

3

Identifying the Hebrew and Greek Words for Patience

Just to give the reader heads up, Chapter 3 and 4 deal more with the stats and technical aspects of patience in the Bible. This will enable the reader to get an overall view of the word "patient" and how it is used in different ways in the Bible.

See the following Strong's Numbers and the word study sentences and the scripture references to follow for the Hebrew word for patience.

We will Deal with 1 Hebrew word for Patience

1) The Hebrew Strong's Number is the Following:

H750 (14x) (slow-9, longsuffering-4, patient)

The first ten passages below are directly referring to God being longsuffering, slow to wrath, or slow to anger and all of these are defining and dealing with patience.

(Exod 34:6) And the LORD passed by before him, and proclaimed, The LORD, The LORD God, merciful and gracious, <u>longsuffering</u>, #750 and abundant in goodness and truth,

(Num 14:18) The LORD is <u>longsuffering</u>, #750 and of great mercy, forgiving iniquity and transgression, and by no means clearing the guilty, visiting the iniquity of the fathers upon the children unto the third and fourth generation.

(Neh 9:17) And refused to obey, neither were mindful of thy wonders that thou didst among them; but hardened their necks, and in their rebellion appointed a captain to return to their bondage: but thou art a God ready to pardon, gracious and merciful, <u>slow #750 to anger</u>, and of great kindness, and forsookest them not.

(Ps 86:15) But thou, O Lord, art a God full of compassion, and gracious, <u>longsuffering, #750</u> and plenteous in mercy and truth.

(Ps 103:8) The LORD is merciful and gracious, <u>slow #750 to anger</u>, and plenteous in mercy.

(Ps 145:8) The LORD is gracious, and full of compassion; <u>slow #750 to anger</u>, and of great mercy.

(Jer 15:15) O LORD, thou knowest: remember me, and visit me, and revenge me of my persecutors; take me not away in thy <u>longsuffering #750</u>: know that for thy sake I have suffered rebuke.

(Joel 2:13) And rend your heart, and not your garments, and turn unto the LORD your God: for he is gracious and merciful, <u>slow #750 to anger</u>, and of great kindness, and repenteth him of the evil.

(Jonah 4:2) And he prayed unto the LORD, and said, I pray thee, O LORD, was not this my saying, when I was yet in my country? Therefore I fled before unto Tarshish: for I knew that thou art a gracious God, and merciful, <u>slow #750 to anger</u>, and of great kindness, and repentest thee of the evil.

(Nah 1:3) The LORD is <u>slow #750 to anger</u>, and great in power, and will not at all acquit the wicked: the LORD hath his way in the whirlwind and in the storm, and the clouds are the dust of his feet.

In the next four passages below God is telling us that mankind should be slow to wrath, or slow to anger, or patient and reap the benefits that come with being so.

(Prov 14:29) He that is <u>slow #750 to wrath</u> is of great understanding: but he that is hasty of spirit exalteth folly.

Notice the contrast of patience or slow to wrath versus haste. The one that is slow to wrath or patient to wrath

13

is of great understanding. Gaining knowledge is directly connected to patience. The impatient and hasty one will exalt folly.

(Prov 15:18) A wrathful man stirreth up strife: but he that is <u>slow #750 to anger</u> appeaseth strife.

The one that is patient to anger will appease or quiet or settle strife. The impatient one will be quick tempered and actually stir up trouble and strife.

(Prov 16:32) He that is <u>slow #750 to anger</u> is better than the mighty; and he that ruleth his spirit than he that taketh a city.

The one that is patient to anger is better than the mighty and able to rule his own spirit. This tell us the great advantage that the patient person will have over everyone else. The patient is better than the mighty.

(Eccl 7:8) Better is the end of a thing than the beginning thereof: and the <u>patient #750</u> in spirit is better than the proud in spirit.

Notice that pride is in contrast and pulls against patience. The individual that has a problem with pride also has a healthy dose of impatience. The individual that has a problem with impatience also has a problem with pride. They seem to go hand in hand.

<u>Now, We will Deal with 7 different
 Greek words for Patience</u>

See the following Strong's Numbers and their word study sentences and the scripture references to follow for the seven Greek words for patience.

1) *G420 (1x)(patient)*

(2Tim 2:24) And the servant of the Lord must not strive; but be gentle unto all men, apt to teach, <u>patient #420</u>,

2) *G1933 (5x)(gentle-3; moderation; patient)*

(Phil 4:5) Let your <u>moderation #1933</u> be known unto all men. The Lord is at hand.

> *Please notice that moderation referred to in this passage is referring to gentleness or patience. It has nothing to do with restraining from the excess of anything. The Bible tells us to totally restrain from anything that is wrong. We according to the Bible are to abstain from the appearance of evil. We are warned that a little can damage a lot. Notice the following passages.*
>
> *(1Thess 5:22) <u>Abstain from all appearance of evil</u>.*
>
> *(1Cor 5:6) Your glorying is not good. Know ye not that <u>a little leaven leaveneth the whole lump</u>?*
>
> *(Gal 5:9) <u>A little leaven leaveneth the whole lump</u>.*

According to Phil 4:5, God is telling us how it is important to display and make known our patience unto all men.

(1Tim 3:3) Not given to wine, no striker, not greedy of filthy lucre; but <u>patient #1933</u>, not a brawler, not covetous;

(Titus 3:2) To speak evil of no man, to be no brawlers, but <u>gentle #1933</u>, shewing all meekness unto all men.

Notice how the gentle or patient one works well with meekness or humility.

(Jas 3:17) But the wisdom that is from above is first pure, then peaceable, <u>gentle #1933</u>, and easy to be intreated, full of mercy and good fruits, without partiality, and without hypocrisy.

(1Pet 2:18) Servants, be subject to your masters with all fear; not only to the good and <u>gentle #1933</u>, but also to the froward.

3) *G3114 (10x)(be patient-3; have patience-2; have long patience; bear long; suffer long; be longsuffering; patiently endure)*

(Matt 18:26) The servant therefore fell down, and worshipped him, saying, Lord, have <u>patience #3114</u> with me, and I will pay thee all.

(Matt 18:29) And his fellowservant fell down at his feet, and besought him, saying, Have <u>patience #3114</u> with me, and I will pay thee all.

(Luke 18:7) And shall not God avenge his own elect, which cry day and night unto him, though he <u>bear long #3114</u> with them?

(1Cor 13:4) Charity <u>suffereth long #3114</u>, and is kind; charity envieth not; charity vaunteth not itself, is not puffed up,

(1Thess 5:14) Now we exhort you, brethren, warn them that are unruly, comfort the feebleminded, support the weak, <u>be patient #3114</u> toward all men.

(Heb 6:15) And so, after he had <u>patiently endured #3114</u>, he obtained the promise.

(Jas 5:7) <u>Be patient #3114</u> therefore, brethren, unto the coming of the Lord. Behold, the husbandman waiteth for the precious fruit of the earth, and hath <u>long patience #3114</u> for it, until he receive the early and latter rain.

(Jas 5:8) Be ye also <u>patient #3114</u>; stablish your hearts: for the coming of the Lord draweth nigh.

(2Pet 3:9) The Lord is not slack concerning his promise, as some men count slackness; but is <u>longsuffering #3114</u> to us-ward, not willing that any should perish, but that all should come to repentance.

4)   *G3115 (14x)(longsuffering-12; patience-2)*

(Rom 2:4) Or despisest thou the riches of his goodness and forbearance and <u>longsuffering #3115</u>; not knowing that the goodness of God leadeth thee to repentance?

(Rom 9:22) What if God, willing to shew his wrath, and to make his power known, endured with much <u>longsuffering #3115</u> the vessels of wrath fitted to destruction:

(2Cor 6:6) By pureness, by knowledge, by <u>longsuffering #3115</u>, by kindness, by the Holy Ghost, by love unfeigned,

(Gal 5:22) But the fruit of the Spirit is love, joy, peace, <u>longsuffering #3115</u>, gentleness, goodness, faith, (Gal 5:23) Meekness, temperance: against such there is no law.

(Eph 4:2) With all lowliness and meekness, with <u>longsuffering #3115</u>, forbearing one another in love;

(Col 1:11) Strengthened with all might, according to his glorious power, unto all <u>patience #5281</u> and <u>longsuffering #3115</u> with joyfulness;

(Col 3:12) Put on therefore, as the elect of God, holy and beloved, bowels of mercies, kindness, humbleness of mind, meekness, <u>longsuffering #3115</u>;

(1Tim 1:16) Howbeit for this cause I obtained mercy, that in me first Jesus Christ might shew forth all <u>longsuffering #3115</u>, for a pattern to them which should hereafter believe on him to life everlasting.

(2Tim 3:10) But thou hast fully known my doctrine, manner of life, purpose, faith, <u>longsuffering #3115</u>, charity, <u>patience #5281</u>,

(2Tim 4:2) Preach the word; be instant in season, out of season; reprove, rebuke, exhort with all <u>longsuffering #3115</u> and doctrine.

(Heb 6:12) That ye be not slothful, but followers of them who through faith and <u>patience #3115</u> inherit the promises.

(Jas 5:10) Take, my brethren, the prophets, who have spoken in the name of the Lord, for an example of suffering affliction, and of <u>patience #3115</u>.

(1Pet 3:20) Which sometime were disobedient, when once the <u>longsuffering #3115</u> of God waited in the days of Noah, while the ark was a preparing, wherein few, that is, eight souls were saved by water.

(2Pet 3:15) And account that the <u>longsuffering #3115</u> of our Lord is salvation; even as our beloved brother Paul also according to the wisdom given unto him hath written unto you;

5) *G3116 (1x)(patiently)*

(Acts 26:3) Especially because I know thee to be expert in all customs and questions which are among the Jews: wherefore I beseech thee to hear me <u>patiently #3116</u>.

6) *G5278 (17x)(endure-11; take patiently-2; tarry behind; abide; patient; suffer)*

(Matt 10:22) And ye shall be hated of all men for my name's sake: but he that <u>endureth #5278</u> to the end shall be saved.

(Matt 24:13) But <u>he that shall endure #5278</u> unto the end, the same shall be saved.

(Mark 13:13) And ye shall be hated of all men for my name's sake: but he that <u>shall endure #5278</u> unto the end, the same shall be saved.

(Luke 2:43) And when they had fulfilled the days, as they returned, the child Jesus <u>tarried behind #5278</u> in Jerusalem; and Joseph and his mother knew not of it.

(Acts 17:14) And then immediately the brethren sent away Paul to go as it were to the sea: but Silas and Timotheus <u>abode</u> there <u>still #5278</u>.

(Rom 12:12) Rejoicing in hope; <u>patient #5278</u> in tribulation; continuing instant in prayer;

(1Cor 13:7) Beareth all things, believeth all things, hopeth all things, <u>endureth #5278</u> all things.

(2Tim 2:10) Therefore I <u>endure #5278</u> all things for the elect's sakes, that they may also obtain the salvation which is in Christ Jesus with eternal glory.

(2Tim 2:12) If we <u>suffer #5278</u>, we shall also reign with him: if we deny him, he also will deny us:

(Heb 10:32) But call to remembrance the former days, in which, after ye were illuminated, ye <u>endured #5278</u> a great fight of afflictions;

(Heb 12:2) Looking unto Jesus the author and finisher of our faith; who for the joy that was set before him <u>endured #5278</u> the cross, despising the shame, and is set down at the right hand of the throne of God.

(Heb 12:3) For consider him that <u>endured #5278</u> such contradiction of sinners against himself, lest ye be wearied and faint in your minds.

(Heb 12:7) If ye <u>endure #5278</u> chastening, God dealeth with you as with sons; for what son is he whom the father chasteneth not?

(Jas 1:12) Blessed is the man that <u>endureth #5278</u> temptation: for when he is tried, he shall receive the crown of life, which the Lord hath promised to them that love him.

(Jas 5:11) Behold, we count them happy which <u>endure. #5278</u> Ye have heard of the patience of Job, and have seen the end of the Lord; that the Lord is very pitiful, and of tender mercy.

(1Pet 2:20) For what glory is it, if, when ye be buffeted for your faults, ye shall take it <u>patiently ? #5278</u> but if, when ye do well, and suffer for it, ye take it <u>patiently, #5278</u> this is acceptable with God.

7) *G5281 (26x)(continuance; enduring; patience-23; waiting)*

(Luke 8:15) But that on the good ground are they, which in an honest and good heart, having heard the word, keep it, and bring forth fruit with <u>patience #5281</u>

(Luke 21:19) In your <u>patience #5281</u> possess ye your souls.

(Rom 2:7) To them who by <u>patient continuance #5281</u> in well doing seek for glory and honour and immortality, eternal life:

(Rom 5:3) And not only so, but we glory in tribulations also: knowing that tribulation worketh <u>patience #5281</u>; (Rom 5:4) And <u>patience #5281</u>, experience; and experience, hope:

(Rom 8:25) But if we hope for that we see not, then do we with <u>patience #5281</u> wait for it.

(Rom 15:4) For whatsoever things were written aforetime were written for our learning, that we through <u>patience #5281</u> and comfort of the scriptures might have hope. (Rom 15:5) Now the God of <u>patience #5281</u> and consolation grant you to be likeminded one toward another according to Christ Jesus:

(2Cor 1:6) And whether we be afflicted, it is for your consolation and salvation, which is effectual in the <u>enduring</u> <u>#5281</u> of the same sufferings which we also suffer: or whether we be comforted, it is for your consolation and salvation.

(2Cor 6:4) But in all things approving ourselves as the ministers of God, in much <u>patience, #5281</u> in afflictions, in necessities, in distresses,

(2Cor 12:12) Truly the signs of an apostle were wrought among you in all <u>patience #5281</u> in signs, and wonders, and mighty deeds.

(Col 1:11) Strengthened with all might, according to his glorious power, unto all <u>patience #5281</u> and <u>longsuffering</u> <u>#3115</u> with joyfulness;

(1Thess 1:3) Remembering without ceasing your work of faith, and labour of love, and <u>patience #5281</u> of hope in our Lord Jesus Christ, in the sight of God and our Father;

(2Thess 1:4) So that we ourselves glory in you in the churches of God for your <u>patience #5281</u> and faith in all your persecutions and tribulations that ye endure:

(2Thess 3:5) And the Lord direct your hearts into the love of God, and into the <u>patient</u> <u>waiting #5281</u> for Christ.

(1Tim 6:11) But thou, O man of God, flee these things; and follow after righteousness, godliness, faith, love, <u>patience, #5281</u> meekness.

(2Tim 3:10) But thou hast fully known my doctrine, manner of life, purpose, faith, <u>longsuffering, #3115</u> charity, <u>patience #5281</u>,

(Titus 2:2) That the aged men be sober, grave, temperate, sound in faith, in charity, in <u>patience. #5281</u>

(Heb 10:36) For ye have need of <u>patience, #5281</u> that, after ye have done the will of God, ye might receive the promise.

(Heb 12:1) Wherefore seeing we also are compassed about with so great a cloud of witnesses, let us lay aside every weight, and the sin which doth so easily beset us, and let us run with <u>patience #5281</u> the race that is set before us,

(Jas 1:3) Knowing this, that the trying of your faith worketh <u>patience #5281</u>. (Jas 1:4) But let <u>patience #5281</u> have her perfect work, that ye may be perfect and entire, wanting nothing.

(Jas 5:11) Behold, we count them happy which <u>endure #5278</u>. Ye have heard of the <u>patience #5281</u> of Job, and have seen the end of the Lord; that the Lord is very pitiful, and of tender mercy.

(2Pet 1:6) And to knowledge temperance; and to temperance <u>patience; #5281</u> and to <u>patience #5281</u> godliness;

(Rev 1:9) I John, who also am your brother, and companion in tribulation, and in the kingdom and <u>patience #5281</u> of Jesus Christ, was in the isle that is called Patmos, for the word of God, and for the testimony of Jesus Christ.

(Rev 2:2) I know thy works, and thy labour, and thy <u>patience #5281</u>, and how thou canst not bear them which are evil: and thou hast tried them which say they are apostles, and are not, and hast found them liars: (Rev 2:3) And hast borne, and hast <u>patience, #5281</u> and for my name's sake hast laboured, and hast not fainted.

(Rev 2:19) I know thy works, and charity, and service, and faith, and thy <u>patience, #5281</u> and thy works; and the last to be more than the first.

(Rev 3:10) Because thou hast kept the word of my <u>patience, #5281</u> I also will keep thee from the hour of temptation, which shall come upon all the world, to try them that dwell upon the earth.

(Rev 13:10) He that leadeth into captivity shall go into captivity: he that killeth with the sword must be killed with the sword. Here is the <u>patience #5281</u> and the faith of the saints.

(Rev 14:12) Here is the <u>patience #5281</u> of the saints: here are they that keep the commandments of God, and the faith of Jesus.

4

Differences Between the Seven Greek Words for Patience

Just to give the reader heads up, Chapter 3 and 4 deal more with the stats and technical aspects of patience in the Bible. This will enable the reader to get an overall view of the word "patient" and how it is used in the Bible.

For us to understand what differences there are between the seven Greek words for patience, we will need to, first of all, show the list again of the Strong's numbers for the Greek words with their part of speech, and their word study sentences put together so we can compare the definitions of each Greek number.

G420 (Adjective) (1x)(patient) 2 Tim 2:24

G1933 (Adjective) (5x)(gentle-3; moderation; patient)

G3114 (Verb) (10x)(be patient-3; have patience-2; have long patience; bear long; suffer long; be longsuffering; patiently endure)

G3115 (Noun) (14x)(longsuffering-12; patience-2)

G3116 (Adverb) (1x)(patiently) Acts 26:3

G5278 (Verb) (17x)(endure-11; take patiently-2; tarry behind; abide; patient; suffer)

G5281 (Noun) (32x)(patient continuance; enduring; patience-29; patient waiting)

The different English words from the King James Bible for each Strong's Number is listed to the right of each Strong's Number and after the part of speech for each Greek word.

Let me remind you that both the King James Bible and the Greek and Hebrew text that it was translated from are preserved and inerrant by God. Since both are preserved and inerrant, every different English word in the King James Bible for each Hebrew or Greek word shown by their Strong's number gives us accurately one-word definitions and short phrase definitions for each Greek or Hebrew word.

Now, we will list the part of speech of each word and the gender of each word as they are used in the King James Bible.

(G420) "patient" in II Tim 2:24 is an adjective in the masculine gender.

G1933 "moderation" in Phil 4:5 is an adjective in the neuter gender.

G1933 "patient" in I Tim 3:3 is an adjective in the masculine gender.

G1933 "gentle" in Titus 3:2 is an adjective in the masculine gender.

G1933 "gentle" in James 3:17 is an adjective in the feminine gender.

G1933 "gentle" in I Pet 2:18 is an adjective in the masculine gender.

Remember because they are all translated from the same Greek word, they typically are all synonyms.

Allow me at this point to inject a brief explanation of the different forms of the six tenses of verbs in the Greek because some will be used for each verb below.

1) The Aorist Tense: is a simple act in the past.
2) The Present Tense: is a continuous and repeating action.
3) The Future Tense: is a simple act that will take place in the future.
4) The Imperfect Tense: is continuous action in the past.
5) The Perfect Tense: is an action or process that occurred in the past and continues through the present and on into the future.

6) The Pluperfect Tense: is like the perfect tense but the results of the action are in the past.

Allow me to elaborate on the present tense to some degree. Technically, there is no such thing as present tense. Because time never stops the present tense has to be continuous. Otherwise, the moment the action stops it immediately becomes the past.

Also, allow me to elaborate somewhat on the "perfect tense." I will give you some examples from the Bible to help you understand the meaning of "perfect tense."

The phrase "it is written" is seen many times in the Bible. The verb "written" is in the perfect tense. Due to this, what is written in the Bible is forever written. The word "saved" in Eph. 2:8 is in the perfect tense. Due to this, when you are saved, you are forever saved. The word "born" in I John 5:1 is in the perfect tense. Due to this, when you are "born of God," you are forever born of God.

The reason this author pointed out these particular two tenses is because many of the verbs in the New Testament are in the present or in the perfect tense. This will help give you more of the impact that the verses in the Bible have with these verbs using those tenses.

The following are a list of verbs and their tenses and the scripture reference. Also, there is a list of the words and the part of speech and their gender.

G3114 "have patience" in Matt 18:26 is a verb in the aorist tense.

G3114 "have patience" in Matt 18:29 is a verb in the aorist tense.

G3114 "bear long" in Luke 18:7 is a verb in the present tense.

G3114 "suffereth long" in I Cor 13:4 is a verb in the present tense.

G3114 "be patient" in I Thess 5:14 is a verb in the present tense.

G3114 "patiently endured" in Heb 6:15 is a verb in the aorist tense.

G3114 "be patient" in James 5:7 is a verb in the aorist tense.

G3114 "hath long patience" in James 5:7 is a verb in the present tense.

G3114 "be patient" in James 5:8 is a verb in the aorist tense.

G3114 "is longsuffering" in 2Pet 3:9 is a verb in the present tense.

G3115 "longsuffering" in Rom 2:4 is a noun in the feminine gender.

G3115 "longsuffering" in Rom 9:2 is a noun in the feminine gender.

G3115 "longsuffering" in II Cor 6:6 is a noun in the feminine gender.

G3115 "longsuffering" in Gal 5:22 is a noun in the feminine gender.

G3115 "longsuffering" in Eph 4:2 is a noun in the feminine gender.

G3115 "longsuffering" in Col 1:11 is a noun in the feminine gender.

G3115 "longsuffering" in Col 3:12 is a noun in the feminine gender.

G3115 "longsuffering" in I Tim 1:16 is a noun in the feminine gender.

G3115 "longsuffering" in II Tim 3:10 is a noun in the feminine gender.

G3115 "longsuffering" in II Tim 4:2 is a noun in the feminine gender.

G3115 "patience" in Heb 6:12 is a noun in the feminine gender.

G3115 "patience" in James 5:10 is a noun in the feminine gender.

G3115 "longsuffering" in I Pet 3:20 is a noun in the feminine gender.

G3115 "longsuffering" in II Pet 3:15 is a noun in the feminine gender.

G3116 "patiently" in Acts 26:3 is an adverb.

G5278 "endureth" in Matt 10:22 is a verb in the aorist tense.

G5278 "shall endure" in Matt 24:13 is a verb in the aorist tense.

G5278 "shall endure" in Mar 13:13 is a verb in the aorist tense.

G5278 "tarried behind" in Luke 2:43 is a verb in the aorist tense.

G5278 "abode still" in Acts 17:14 is a verb in the imperfect tense.

G5278 "patient" in Rom 12:12 is a verb in the present tense.

G5278 "endureth" in I Cor 13:7 is a verb in the present tense.

G5278 "endure" in II Tim 2:10 is a verb in the present tense.

G5278 "suffer" in II Tim 2:12 is a verb in the present tense.

G5278 "endured" in Heb 10:32 is a verb in the aorist tense.

G5278 "endured" in Heb 12:2 is a verb in the aorist tense.

G5278 "endured" in Heb 12:3 is a verb in the <u>perfect tense</u>.

G5278 "endure" in Heb 12:7 is a verb in the present tense.

G5278 "endureth" in James 1:12 is a verb in the present tense.

G5278 "which endure" in James 5:11 is a verb in the present tense.

G5278 "take patiently" in I Pet 2:20 is a verb in the future tense.

G5278 "take patiently" in I Pet 2:20 is a verb in the future tense.

G5281 "patience" in Luke 8:15 is a noun in the feminine gender.

G5281 "patience" in Luke 21:19 is a noun in the feminine gender.

G5281 "patient continuance" in Rom 2:7 is a noun in the feminine gender.

G5281 "patience" in Rom 5:3 is a noun in the feminine gender.

G5281 "patience" in Rom 5:4 is a noun in the feminine gender.

G5281 "patience" in Rom 8:25 is a noun in the feminine gender.

G5281 "patience" in Rom 15:4 is a noun in the feminine gender.

G5281 "patience" in Rom 15:5 is a noun in the feminine gender.

G5281 "enduring" in 2Cor 1:6 is a noun in the feminine gender.

G5281 "patience" in 2Cor 6:4 is a noun in the feminine gender.

G5281 "patience" in 2Cor 12:12 is a noun in the feminine gender.

G5281 "patience" in Col 1:11 is a noun in the feminine gender.

G5281 "patience" in I Thess 1:3 is a noun in the feminine gender.

G5281 "patience" in II Thess 1:4 is a noun in the feminine gender.

G5281 "patient waiting" in II Thess 3:5 is a noun in the feminine gender.

G5281 "patience" in I Tim 6:11 is a noun in the feminine gender.

G5281 "patience" in II Tim 3:10 is a noun in the feminine gender.

G5281 "patience" in Titus 2:2 is a noun in the feminine gender.

G5281 "patience" in Heb 10:36 is a noun in the feminine gender.

G5281 "patience" in Heb 12:1 is a noun in the feminine gender.

G5281 "patience" in James 1:3 is a noun in the feminine gender.

G5281 "patience" in James 1:4 is a noun in the feminine gender.

G5281 "patience" in James 5:11 is a noun in the feminine gender.

G5281 "patience" in II Pet 1:6 is a noun in the feminine gender.

G5281 "patience" in II Pet 1:6 is a noun in the feminine gender.

G5281 "patience" in Rev 1:9 is a noun in the feminine gender.

G5281 "patience" in Rev 2:2 is a noun in the feminine gender.

G5281 "patience" in Rev 2:3 is a noun in the feminine gender.

G5281 "patience" in Rev 2:19 is a noun in the feminine gender.

G5281 "patience" in Rev 3:10 is a noun in the feminine gender.

G5281 "patience" in Rev 13:10 is a noun in the feminine gender.

G5281 "patience" in Rev 14:12 is a noun in the feminine gender.

The summary of the parts of speech for each Greek word and Strong's Number is as follows: G420 is an Adjective; Every G1933 is an Adjective; Every G3114 is a Verb; Every G3115 is a Noun; G3116 is an Adverb; Every G5278 is a Verb; and Every G5281 is a Noun.

It needs to be pointed out that 3114, 3115, and 3116 all are a set that stems from the same root word but each number deals with a different part of speech of the same Greek word. 3114 is a Verb. 3115 is a noun and 3116 is an adverb.

5278 and 5281 are also a set that stems from the same root word and each number deals with a different part of speech of the same Greek word. 5278 is a verb and 5281 is a noun.

There are passages in the New Testament that have some of the different Greek words for the word, patience, in the same passage. This indicates that there is some difference between the words that we need to be aware of. Notice the following passages.

(Col 1:11) Strengthened with all might, according to his glorious power, unto all patience #5281 and longsuffering #3115 with joyfulness;
    Note: Both #5281 and #3115 are nouns.

(2Tim 3:10) But thou hast fully known my doctrine, manner of life, purpose, faith, longsuffering, #3115 charity, patience #5281,
    Note: Both #5281 and #3115 are nouns.

(Jas 5:11) Behold, we count them happy which <u>endure</u> <u>#5278</u>. Ye have heard of the <u>patience</u> <u>#5281</u> of Job, and have seen the end of the Lord; that the Lord is very pitiful, and of tender mercy.

Note: #5278 is a verb and #5281 is a noun.

Now, let's single out the two nouns in the group.

G5281 (Noun) (32x)(patient continuance; enduring; patience-29; patient waiting)

G5281 is typically the act of peacefully waiting for something to pass. In other words, it is in the present and you are waiting for some condition or person or place or thing to pass. An example would be that you are presently in a trial and you are waiting for the trial to pass. This helps us to see why the English word, "enduring," shows up in the word study sentence above for G5281.

G3115 (Noun) (14x)(longsuffering-12; patience-2)

G3115 is typically the act of peacefully waiting for something to come. In other words, it is in the future and you are waiting for it to come. An example would be that you have ask God to meet a need and you are waiting for the need to be met or as another example you are patiently waiting, as should be true for every living believer, for Jesus to come back. This helps us to see why the English word, "longsuffering," shows up in the word study sentence above for G3115.

5

The God of Patience

(Rom 15:5) Now the <u>God of patience</u> and consolation grant you to be likeminded one toward another according to Christ Jesus:

> *To be likeminded one toward another we must use the Bible as our common denominator for faith and practice but also, we must have the God of patience for our help.*

> *The following verses below speak volumes in themselves of the wonderful, and holy, and powerful God we have who, amazing as it is, is patient with the very fragile, and sinful creatures that we are.*

> *Each believer can speak from personal experience of how patient God is with them. <u>For the believer to be God like or godly, they are going to have to be patient.</u>*

(Exod 34:6) And the LORD passed by before him, and proclaimed, <u>The LORD, The LORD God, merciful and</u>

gracious, longsuffering #750, and abundant in goodness and truth,

(Num 14:18) The LORD is longsuffering #750, and of great mercy, forgiving iniquity and transgression, and by no means clearing the guilty, visiting the iniquity of the fathers upon the children unto the third and fourth generation.

(Neh 9:17) And refused to obey, neither were mindful of thy wonders that thou didst among them; but hardened their necks, and in their rebellion appointed a captain to return to their bondage: but thou art a God ready to pardon, gracious and merciful, slow #750 to anger, and of great kindness, and forsookest them not.

(Ps 86:15) But thou, O Lord, art a God full of compassion, and gracious, longsuffering #750, and plenteous in mercy and truth.

(Ps 103:8) The LORD is merciful and gracious, slow #750 to anger, and plenteous in mercy.

(Ps 145:8) The LORD is gracious, and full of compassion; slow #750 to anger, and of great mercy.

(Jer 15:15) O LORD, thou knowest: remember me, and visit me, and revenge me of my persecutors; take me not away in thy longsuffering #750: know that for thy sake I have suffered rebuke.

(Joel 2:13) And rend your heart, and not your garments, and turn unto the LORD your God: for he is gracious and merciful, <u>slow #750 to anger</u>, and of great kindness, and repenteth him of the evil.

(Jonah 4:2) And he prayed unto the LORD, and said, I pray thee, O LORD, was not this my saying, when I was yet in my country? Therefore I fled before unto Tarshish: for I knew that thou art a gracious God, and merciful, <u>slow #750 to anger</u>, and of great kindness, and repentest thee of the evil.

(Nah 1:3) The LORD is <u>slow #750 to anger</u>, and great in power, and will not at all acquit the wicked: the LORD hath his way in the whirlwind and in the storm, and the clouds are the dust of his feet.

(1Tim 1:16) Howbeit for this cause I obtained mercy, that in me first <u>Jesus Christ might shew forth all longsuffering #3115, for a pattern to them which should hereafter believe on him to life everlasting.</u>

> *What an amazing example God has set for every believer in God's longsuffering. Again, for the believer to be God like or godly, he is going to have to be longsuffering or patient.*

(Jas 5:7) Be <u>patient #3114</u> therefore, brethren, unto the coming of the Lord. Behold, <u>the husbandman waiteth for the precious fruit of the earth, and hath long patience #3114 for it</u>, until he receive the early and latter rain.

God is patiently waiting for the people that will get saved to be saved. As God is patient so should we be patiently witnessing and waiting for people to get saved and for Jesus to return.

(1Pet 3:20) Which sometime were disobedient, when once <u>the longsuffering #3115 of God</u> <u>waited in the days of Noah</u>, while the ark was a preparing, wherein few, that is, eight souls were saved by water.

Can you imagine the patience of God where only eight people out of the entire world population were saved? The rest of the population rejected Christ at their choice.

(2Pet 3:9) The Lord is not slack concerning his promise, as some men count slackness; but <u>is longsuffering #3114 to us-ward, not willing that any should perish, but that all should come to repentance.</u>

God patiently gives everyone a chance to put their faith in Christ to be saved.

(2Pet 3:15) And account that <u>the longsuffering #3115 of our Lord is salvation</u>; even as our beloved brother Paul also according to the wisdom given unto him hath written unto you;

It is because of God's longsuffering that anyone has the opportunity to be saved. Very few people get saved the first time they hear the gospel.

Once again, <u>if you are going to be godly, you are going to have to be patient</u>.

6

How Patience is Acquired

Some of the Tools God uses to Produce Patience in the Believer

One of the things that this author has heard even from his youth from many individuals is the following statement. "Never pray for patience because God will send tribulation into your life to produce the patience." It is true according to the Bible, one of the tools that God uses to produce patience in the believer is trials and tribulations in your life. However, this is not the only tool that God uses to produce patience in the believer.

Notice the following passages and statements for the different tools that God uses to produce patience in each believer.

1) Tribulations

(Rom 5:3) And not only so, but we glory in tribulations also: knowing that <u>tribulation worketh patience</u>; (Rom

5:4) And <u>patience</u>, experience; and experience, hope: (Rom 5:5) And hope maketh not ashamed; because the love of God is shed abroad in our hearts by the Holy Ghost which is given unto us.

You will notice according to the divine order above, before you can gain experience, you will have to go through patience and before you gain patience you will have to go through tribulations. The person that has no patience will gain no experience. We must be pulled from our comfort zone before we can gain patience or experience or even know what real hope is. Remember that hope is faith projected into the future.

It is also worth pointing out at this time the word study sentence for the word "experience." It is as follows:

Experience G1381 (7x)(experience-2; experiment; proof-3; <u>trial</u>)

Notice that the word "trial" is in the list of words for G1381. This is telling us that experience is a trial that has been patiently and successfully lived.

When God gets the believer through one trial, then the believer will realize that God will get him through any and all trials. Because the believer knows that God has got him through the trials in life, the believer gains the patience and assurance that God will get him through any trial. This produces the hope that God does all things well and cannot and will not fail in their personal lives.

(Rom 8:28) And <u>we know that all things work together for good to them that love God, to them who are the called according to *his* purpose</u>.

The believer would be wise to take notes and learn as much as possible from each trial that comes his way. This not only prepares him better for the next trial, this also equips the believer to help other believers in their trials that they are going through. The wise believer will make the trials he goes through a learning experience. Remember, all trials are a time of learning and growing.

2) The Trying of your Faith

(Jas 1:3) Knowing this, that <u>the trying of your faith worketh patience</u>. (Jas 1:4) But <u>let patience have her perfect work</u>, that ye may be perfect and entire, wanting nothing.

According to the above passage, for you to be complete and entire and needing nothing you will have to have patience and in order to have patience your faith must be tested and tried. The testing and trying of your faith will also cause you to dig deeper in your Bible which will strengthen your faith. Allow me to put the trying of your faith in different words. In order for patience to be cultivated your faith is going to have to be challenged. God will providentially do this in many different ways. We must also remember the source of our faith. Notice the following passage.

(Rom 10:17) So then faith *cometh* by hearing, and hearing by the word of God.

In order to strengthen the believer, God will providentially allow everything that he believes to be challenged. This will cause the believer to go deeper and deeper into the scriptures to back up what he believes. In this process he will purge out the things that he believes that cannot be backed up with the scripture and strengthen everything that he believes that are backed up with the Bible with even more Bible verses.

3) Humility

(Eccl 7:8) Better is the end of a thing than the beginning thereof: and <u>the patient in spirit is better than the proud in spirit.</u>

Another tool that helps bring patience to the individual is humility. According to the passage above, pride seems to do away with and pull against patience and actually produces and strengthens impatience. That being the case, it makes since that humility would aid in bringing and producing patience in the believer's life.

One of the things you will notice about pride is that it is very impatient. No doubt, the person that has a problem with pride, also has a problem trying to be patient and the person that has a problem with impatience also has a problem with pride. Notice the following passages.

(2Chr 33:12) And when he was in affliction, he besought the LORD his God, and <u>humbled himself greatly before the God</u> of his fathers,

(Mic 6:8) He hath shewed thee, O man, what *is* good; and <u>what doth the LORD require of thee, but to do justly, and to love mercy, and to walk humbly with thy God?</u>

(1Pet 5:5) Likewise, ye younger, submit yourselves unto the elder. Yea, all *of you* be subject one to another, and <u>be clothed with humility: for God resisteth the proud, and giveth grace to the humble.</u> (1Pet 5:6) <u>Humble yourselves therefore under the mighty hand of God, that he may exalt you in due time:</u>

4) Faith, Virtue, Knowledge, and Temperance

Still another tool that helps bring patience into your life is as you allow God to cultivate and improve your character as a believer. Notice the following.

(2Pet 1:5) And beside this, giving all diligence, add to your <u>faith</u> virtue; and to <u>virtue</u> knowledge; (2Pet 1:6) And to <u>knowledge</u> temperance; and to <u>temperance</u> patience; and to <u>patience</u> godliness; (2Pet 1:7) And to <u>godliness</u> brotherly kindness; and to <u>brotherly kindness</u> charity.

Notice the divine order above. First there has to be faith, then virtue, then knowledge and then temperance and then patience. A believer will have to have faith, virtue, knowledge, and temperance before he is able to develop patience as he should. After patience then comes godliness, brotherly kindness and charity. As has already been said previously, <u>if you are going to be godly you are going to have to be patient</u>.

One of the scary things about pride is that it has a tendency to blind you of your real needs. Notice the following passage.

(Rev 3:17) Because thou sayest, I am rich, and increased with goods, and have need of nothing; and knowest not that thou art wretched, and miserable, and poor, and blind, and naked:

5) Love

It seems that charity is the final goal for the cultivation of the believer's character. Be aware that charity is unconditional love. That being said, notice the following passages of scripture that tell us that even the goal of the law of God is to produce unconditional love in the believer.

(Rom 13:8) Owe no man anything, but to love one another: for <u>he that loveth another hath fulfilled the law.</u>

(Rom 13:10) Love worketh no ill to his neighbour: therefore <u>love is the fulfilling of the law.</u>

(Gal 5:14) For <u>all the law is fulfilled in one word, even in this; Thou shalt love thy neighbour as thyself.</u>

(Jas 2:8) If ye <u>fulfil the royal law according to the scripture,</u> <u>Thou shalt love thy neighbour as thyself,</u> ye do well:

In order to develop unconditional love in your character you are going to have to go through patience. Having said this about love or charity, there is a special characteristic in charity that needs to be pointed out. Notice the following passage.

(1Cor 13:1) Though I speak with the tongues of men and of angels, and have not charity, I am become as sounding brass, or a tinkling cymbal. (1Cor 13:2) And though I have the gift of prophecy, and understand all mysteries, and all knowledge; and though I have all faith, so that I could remove mountains, and have not charity, I am nothing. (1Cor 13:3) And though I bestow all my goods to feed the poor, and though I give my body to be burned, and have not charity, it profiteth me nothing. (1Cor 13:4) <u>Charity suffereth long, #3114</u> and is kind; charity envieth not; charity vaunteth not itself, is not puffed up, (1Cor 13:5) Doth not behave itself unseemly, seeketh not her own, is not easily provoked, thinketh no evil; (1Cor 13:6) Rejoiceth not in iniquity, but rejoiceth in the truth; (1Cor 13:7) Beareth all things, believeth all things, hopeth all things, <u>endureth #5278</u> <u>all things</u>.

One of the qualities in charity or love is "<u>suffereth long</u>" <u>#3114</u> and also "endureth" #5278 all things. These two words are also from the list of Greek Strong's numbers meaning "<u>patient</u>." So, with this in mind, as we allow God to cultivate unconditional love in our lives, you will have to go through patience. In turn this will help the believer to be more patient with the unbeliever and the believer in helping them to overcome sins in their lives.

> (Prov 10:12) Hatred stirreth up strifes: but <u>love covereth all sins</u>.
>
> (Prov 17:9) <u>He that covereth a transgression seeketh love</u>; but he that repeateth a matter separateth *very* friends.
>
> (Gal 6:1) Brethren, if a man be overtaken in a fault, ye which are spiritual, restore such an one in the spirit of meekness; considering thyself, lest thou also be tempted.

You perhaps have noticed that the one that typically is the most patient with the handicapped individual is the mother of the handicapped individual. The love from the mother brings out the patience to help the helpless and work tirelessly with the special child when very few other people will.

6) Learning from the Experience of Others in the Scriptures

(Rom 15:4) For whatsoever things were written aforetime were written for our learning, that we through <u>patience #5281</u> and comfort of the scriptures might have hope.

There should be no surprise that the study of the scriptures will also cultivate patience in our lives. Through the stories and instructions that God gives us in the Bible, we will progressively build patience more and more. As we read about the mistakes that previous believers in the Bible have made, we will surely learn from their mistakes and not use them as an excuse or cop-out to repeat their mistakes. Not only does faith come by hearing the Word of God (Rom 10:17), no doubt, patience also comes by studying the Word of God.

(2Tim 2:15) Study to shew thyself approved unto God, a workman that needeth not to be ashamed, rightly dividing the word of truth.

7

Patience versus the Temper

Perhaps you are wondering, what does patience have to do with your temper? The short answer is everything. In the Old Testament passages below, the English word "slow" in the phrase "slow to wrath," is the same as the Hebrew word #750 which is also translated in the KJV as "patient." So, the phrase could also read "patient to wrath." Of the many things that are wrong about a bad temper, one of them is that <u>a bad temper is a visible and sometimes verbal and open display of the absence of patience.</u> It is almost endless how much damage a believer with a bad temper will cause.

God Sets the Example
God is Slow to Wrath or Patient to be Angry

(Neh 9:17) And refused to obey, neither were mindful of thy wonders that thou didst among them; but hardened their necks, and in their rebellion appointed a captain to return to their bondage: but <u>thou art a God</u> ready to pardon, gracious and merciful, <u>slow #750 to anger</u>, and of great kindness, and forsookest them not.

(Ps 103:8) <u>The LORD is</u> merciful and gracious, <u>slow #750 to anger</u>, and plenteous in mercy.

(Ps 145:8) <u>The LORD is</u> gracious, and full of compassion; <u>slow #750 to anger</u>, and of great mercy.

(Joel 2:13) And rend your heart, and not your garments, and turn unto <u>the LORD your God: for he is</u> gracious and merciful, <u>slow #750 to anger</u>, and of great kindness, and repenteth him of the evil.

(Jonah 4:2) And he prayed unto the LORD, and said, I pray thee, O LORD, was not this my saying, when I was yet in my country? Therefore I fled before unto Tarshish: for I knew that <u>thou art a gracious God</u>, and merciful, <u>slow #750 to anger</u>, and of great kindness, and repentest thee of the evil.

(Nah 1:3) <u>The LORD is slow #750 to anger</u>, and great in power, and will not at all acquit the wicked: the LORD hath his way in the whirlwind and in the storm, and the clouds are the dust of his feet.

The Following is a Summary of
a Temper versus Patience

First, the Patient Believer Who Controls His Temper.

A) He is of great understanding.

(Prov 14:29) <u>He that is slow #750 to wrath is of great understnding</u>: but he that is hasty of spirit exalteth folly.

B) He is able to appease strife

(Prov 15:18) A wrathful man stirreth up strife: but he that is <u>slow #750 to anger</u> <u>appeaseth strife</u>.

Note: "appeaseth" H8252 (41x)(rest-16; quiet-16; quietness-4; still-2; appeaseth; idleness; settled)

With patience you are able to quieten down and settle the strife at hand. Notice the following passage.

(Matt 5:9) <u>Blessed *are* the peacemakers: for they shall be called the children of God</u>.

C) He is better than the mighty.

(Prov 16:32) He that is <u>slow #750 to anger</u> <u>is better than the mighty</u>; and he that ruleth his spirit than he that taketh a city.

Second, the Impatient Believer with a Bad Temper

A) The believer is instructed not to stay angry with the following warnings.

1) Let not the sun go down upon your wrath.

(Eph 4:26) Be ye angry, and sin not: <u>let not the sun go down upon your wrath</u>:

2) Anger rests in the bosom of fools.

(Eccl 7:9) Be not hasty in thy spirit to be angry: for <u>anger resteth in the bosom of fools</u>.

B) The temper can lead the believer into further sin.

1) Be ye angry and sin not.

(Eph 4:26) <u>Be ye angry, and sin not</u>: let not the sun go down upon your wrath:

2) An angry man stirs up strife, and a furious man abounds in transgression.

(Prov 29:22) <u>An angry man stirreth up strife, and a furious man aboundeth in transgression.</u>

C) The temper can cause the believer to do very foolish things.

1) He that is soon angry deals foolishly.

(Prov 14:17) <u>*He that is* soon angry dealeth foolishly</u>: and a man of wicked devices is hated.

    2) He that is hasty of spirit exalts folly.

(Prov 14:29) He that is slow to wrath is of great understanding: but <u>he that is hasty of spirit exalteth folly.</u>

    D) The temper can bring due punishment upon the impatient believer.

        1) A man of great wrath shall suffer punishment.

(Prov 19:19) <u>A man of great wrath shall suffer punishment</u>: for if thou deliver *him*, yet thou must do it again.

    Third, What God says to do When Encountering Others with a Bad Temper

(Prov 15:1) A soft answer turneth away wrath: but grievous words stir up anger.

One of the worst things you can do is get drawn into an argument with someone over any issue and especially out in the general public. Horrifying it will be when the volumes are raised, and it turns into a shouting match. Your testimony is damaged, and everyone loses. You are not put in that situation by God to win an argument. You are put in that situation to help the individual.

(Prov 13:10) <u>Only by pride cometh contention</u>: but with the well advised *is* wisdom.

When the individual you are addressing is presently in a hot display of a temper, it would be a good time to give them space and let them cool down. Notice the following passage of scripture.

(Prov 22:24) Make no friendship with an angry man; and with a furious man thou shalt not go:

In the above passage, God is not telling us to be unfriendly. He is warning us to avoid the influence of the temper of others but not to avoid others. The temper is very contagious. While men are angry, we need to give them space until they can cool down. Remember, "a soft answer turneth away wrath."

(Prov 30:33) Surely the churning of milk bringeth forth butter, and the wringing of the nose bringeth forth blood: so <u>the forcing of wrath bringeth forth strife</u>.

With God given patience you will be given the strength, character, and heart to control your temper even in spite of the anger and temper of others.

(Jas 1:19) Wherefore, my beloved brethren, let every man be swift to hear, slow to speak, <u>slow to wrath</u>:

8

Patience versus Listening

(Acts 26:3) Especially because I know thee to be expert in all customs and questions which are among the Jews: wherefore I beseech thee to <u>hear me patiently</u>.

Perhaps the question will come up that says, "How are hearing or listening and patience connected?"

Allow me to explain and illustrate. When a person is involved in a one on one conversation or let us say we have a situation when there is a person that is involved in listening to a person that is preaching or teaching or giving out information with a question and answer time following the session. The impatient listener is many times thinking of a question or a statement to make while the speaker is talking so the listener is thinking of something else instead of listening to the speaker. That is the tendency of an impatient listener. The impatient listener will not be focused on what is being said, so, the impatient listener will not hear and will not learn from what is being taught. The person that dares to interrupt the speaker is definitely an impatient listener.

A good example of impatient listening is in your typical newsroom. Typically, the reporters are so focused on getting their questions asked that they have already written down, that they are not listening to what is being said or has been said to the other reporters. Proof of this is that many reporters ask the same question over and over when they have already been "asked and answered."

The person that is impatient does not have ears to hear. Jesus made this statement at least eight times in the Bible. Notice the following passages.

(Matt 11:15) He that hath ears to hear, let him hear.

(Matt 13:9) Who hath ears to hear, let him hear.

(Matt 13:43) Then shall the righteous shine forth as the sun in the kingdom of their Father. Who hath ears to hear, let him hear.

(Mark 4:9) And he said unto them, He that hath ears to hear, let him hear.

(Mark 4:23) If any man have ears to hear, let him hear.

(Mark 7:16) If any man have ears to hear, let him hear.

(Luke 8:8) And other fell on good ground, and sprang up, and bare fruit an hundredfold. And when he had said these things, he cried, <u>He that hath ears to hear, let him hear</u>.

(Luke 14:35) It is neither fit for the land, nor yet for the dunghill; but men cast it out. <u>He that hath ears to hear, let him hear.</u>

Jesus is not referring to people that do not have the ability to hear. He is referring to people who do not have the will to hear. The lack of patience will hinder and even stop a person from hearing which destroys that particular opportunity to gain information and learn.

As has already been said, pride produces impatience and a person that thinks he knows more than the speaker on a given subject will have a hard time listening and learning anymore on that subject due to the absence of humility and patience.

God has given every human a very powerful mind. The capability of the human brain is almost impossible to measure. With all that capability, it may be hard to believe that in spite of the speed of the thoughts in the brain, the brain can only produce one thought at a time. Because of the ability that the brain has to put out such a high speed of thoughts we typically have a hard time focusing on one topic at a time.

If you are not listening and focused on what the speaker is saying, you are not going to learn from the speaker because your mind is racing elsewhere.

Perhaps you might have met individuals who are so impatient with their listening that they have a tendency to try to answer a question before the question is completely asked. Notice the following passages.

(Prov 18:13) He that answereth a matter before he heareth *it*, it *is* folly and shame unto him.

(Prov 15:28) <u>The heart of the righteous studieth to answer</u>: but the mouth of the wicked poureth out evil things.

(Prov 20:12) <u>The hearing ear, and the seeing eye, the LORD hath made even both of them.</u>

(Jas 1:19) Wherefore, my beloved brethren, <u>let every man be swift to hear, slow to speak,</u> slow to wrath:

Perhaps you have heard the old saying that goes as follow. I have two ears and one mouth. I must strive to make the amount of hearing double the amount of speaking.

9

Patience versus Running

(Heb 12:1) Wherefore seeing we also are compassed about with so great a cloud of witnesses, let us lay aside every weight, and the sin which doth so easily beset us, and let us <u>run with patience</u> the race that is set before us,

It almost seems like a conflict in terms to put running together with patience. The individual that is running is typically the one that is in a hurry and operating with very little time and even less patience.

You may be thinking about the story of "The Tortoise and the Hare." Yes, the turtle displayed a lot more patience than did the rabbit. Technically though, the turtle's pace does not qualify as running.

Allow me to use some illustrations from my past that might show how running and patience go together.

In running track, known to most, there are two different kinds of runners typically on the track field. Woe be unto the track team that has a coach that does not know this. At the beginning of the season to get his runners into shape the coach who knows nothing of the two types of runners would put everyone running long distances. Unknown to some coaches is the fact that the sprinter gets in shape by running sprints and the long-distance runner gets in shape by running long distances. Notice the following details.

The sprinter is the one that would run in the 100 Yard Dash, the 220 Yard Dash, the 440 Yard Dash, and the 440 Yard Relay. This was the type of races that this author would run back in his younger days in school. The race would be quick, and the runner must put everything he has into that quick race and have nothing left when he crosses the finish line. The race happens very fast and is over in seconds.

Then there is the long-distance runner. This is the one that will have to run with patience. This runner's pace must be measured carefully and even his breathing must be carefully distributed throughout the length of the entire race. Back in the old days, the distance-runner would run in the 880 and in the Mile and 2 Mile races and some would run marathons of great distances.

When God used the illustration of running with patience in Hebrews 12:1, he was referring to the distance-runner and not to the sprinter. The distance of this race is from the moment of salvation all the way to the death of the believer or until Jesus comes to get the believer.

We have in the ministry a lot of sprinters instead of long-distant runners who turn out to be "flashes in a pan" and "over-night-ers." They fizzle out not realizing that the race in the ministry must be run with patience. They want to set the woods on fire but wind up putting their own candle out. If they do not have a healthy dose of patience they will give up or even quit the ministry.

The condition of running with patience or distant running is described in the passage below.

(Isa 40:31) But they that wait upon the LORD shall renew *their* strength; they shall mount up with wings as eagles; they shall run, and not be weary; *and* they shall walk, and not faint.

Please allow me to use a second experience in sports from my past. It is in the game of racquetball. This game over all is an extremely fast paced game. Back in the old days the sports world was reluctant to televise it because the sport was extremely fast and was very difficult to set up cameras and a lengthy televised schedule for the game.

The experienced racquetball player knew that in spite of the speed of the game, the player must be very patient in his playing. For example, the impatient player would hit the ball with his racquet while the ball was too high from the floor. This would easily set up his opponent for what is called a kill shot that could not be returned. The impatient player will hit the ball simply because he can reach it instead of waiting until the ball gets closer to the floor and in a better position. The impatient player would run after the ball instead of running to where the ball is going in order to intercept the ball. Trust me. You will run out of energy quick, trying to chase a racquet ball. The impatient player would waste his energy and would lose the game in fatigue to the patient player.

Still another illustration that might help is the process of firing a rifle. Years ago, I had the privilege of leading a man to Christ. The man was a retired Marine Sniper. He had many amazing stories to tell. To hear him give details about how to shoot a rifle was quite interesting. He would never use the phrase, "pull the trigger" when referring to firing the rifle. As a matter of fact, he would get quite upset with anyone that used the phrase, "pull the trigger." The individual that pulls the trigger will have the tendency to jerk the trigger and in turn jerk the rifle and scope away from the target. His correct term would be to "squeeze the trigger." He would make it clear that the impatient shooter that pulls the trigger would not be able to hit the side of a barn. The patient shooter would squeeze the trigger of the rifle slowly while slowly exhaling the air from his lungs. This process would keep the crosshairs on the target while firing the weapon and the result would be that the target was hit. The patient man slowly squeezes the trigger and the impatient man will pull the trigger too quickly and move the crosshairs off the target and miss the shot and even perhaps the side of a barn.

From these illustrations we can see the value of running with patience. We can see from the illustrations above that even fast things require patience. Now since the running is compared with serving God by serving people, we can understand how valuable patience is in every part of our service.

Only the patient runner will finish the race well.

(2Tim 4:7) I have fought a good fight, <u>I have finished *my* course</u>, I have kept the faith:

Finishing Well

As years go by and days pass on
It is clear to see that time is almost gone.

Traveling in the river of life and coming to a bend
More and more things in life are pointing to the end.

With signs all around us that we are
winding down it is easy to tell
This is why we must see the urgency
and importance of finishing well.

In spite of a rough start through the storms
in the sea of life we can recover

As we go through life and are coming to
the end, we will then soon discover

The testimony that is displayed with the
courage and grit of finishing well.
Even people will remember the finish more
than the times in life that we fell.

It is important to see in spite of the
stumbling in life you would not quit
You stayed with it and did what you could
and on the bench, you refused to sit.

With serving God with all your might
and sometimes you made a flop
It was not giving up or quitting, but it was
death that could only cause you to stop.

Upon hearing God say, "Well done" to
the good and faithful He will tell
Even in those two words we see the value
that God places on finishing well.

(1Cor 9:24) Know ye not that they which run in a race run all, but one receiveth the prize? So run, that ye may obtain.

10

Patience with Our Fellow Humans

(1Thess 5:14) Now we exhort you, brethren, warn them that are unruly, comfort the feebleminded, support the weak, <u>be patient toward all men.</u>

The phrase, "be patient toward all men" is a command from God's word and not just a mere suggestion. We must warn and comfort and support humanity with patience. We must be patient with the unruly, the feebleminded, and the weak. To be patient toward all men includes unbelievers, believers, young and old, rich and poor, and even our self. This also includes your kin, your wife or husband, your children, your boss, your co-workers, and even your enemies. They like we are all human.

The most valuable thing on the planet is the human. The human is the only one on the planet that is created in the image of God. The human is the only one that Jesus suffered and bled and died for to save them from Hell. The human is the only one on the planet that possesses an eternal soul. However, the human has been given by God the ability to choose, whether he chooses right or chooses wrong. According to the Bible, at the human's choice, the majority of humans will reject Christ as Savior and perish in the lake of fire for eternity. Notice the following passage.

(Matt 7:13) Enter ye in at the strait gate: for wide is the gate, and broad is the way, that leadeth to destruction, and <u>many there be which go in there at</u>: (Matt 7:14) Because strait is the gate, and narrow is the way, which leadeth unto life, and <u>few there be that find it.</u>

Even though salvation is free to all, salvation can only be seen in and through the scriptures.

(Rom 10:17) So then <u>faith cometh by hearing, and hearing by the word of God.</u>

So, the majority of the human race will refuse to believe the Bible and reject Jesus as their personal Savior. Keep in mind that their very soul is at stake. How we, the believers, handle ourselves around the unbeliever and how we handle the unbeliever is of the greatest importance. Even when the believer is mistreated by the unbeliever, we catch ourselves wanting to retaliate and to impatiently take matters into our own hands. Are we foolishly worried that the unbeliever's Hell is not going to be bad enough? Jesus was very clear on how we are to treat the unbeliever. Notice the following.

(Matt 5:44) But I say unto you, <u>Love your enemies, bless them that curse you, do good to them that hate you, and pray for them which despitefully use you, and persecute you;</u>

(Luke 6:27) But I say unto you which hear, <u>Love your enemies, do good to them which hate you</u>, (Luke 6:28) <u>Bless them that curse you, and pray for them which despitefully use you.</u> (Luke 6:29) And unto him that smiteth thee on the *one* cheek offer also the other; and him that taketh away thy cloke forbid not *to take thy* coat also. (Luke 6:30) Give to every man that asketh of thee; and of him that taketh away thy goods ask *them* not again. (Luke 6:31) And <u>as ye would that men should do to you, do ye also to them likewise.</u> (Luke 6:32) For if ye love them which love you, what thank have ye? for sinners also love those that love them. (Luke 6:33) And if ye do good to them which do good to you, what thank have ye? for sinners also do even the same. (Luke 6:34) And if ye lend *to them* of whom ye hope to receive, what thank have ye? for sinners also lend to sinners, to receive as much again. (Luke 6:35) But love ye your enemies, and do good, and lend, hoping for nothing again; and your reward shall be great, and ye shall be the children of the Highest: for he is kind unto the unthankful and *to* the evil. (Luke 6:36) Be ye therefore merciful, as your Father also is merciful.

For a believer to walk through this life with impatience toward unbelievers, it would be impossible to measure the damage that they would cause. Notice the following passage.

(2Cor 3:2) <u>Ye are our epistle written in our hearts, known and read of all men</u>: (2Cor 3:3) Forasmuch as ye are manifestly declared to be the epistle of Christ ministered by us, written not with ink, but with the Spirit of the living God; not in tables of stone, but in fleshy tables of the heart.

(2Tim 2:25) <u>In meekness instructing those that oppose themselves;</u> if God peradventure will give them repentance to the acknowledging of the truth;

(Phil 4:5) Let your <u>moderation #1933</u> be known unto all men. The Lord is at hand.

God gives us His perspective of the believer in this lost and dying world and how we should handle ourselves. Notice the following passages.

(Matt 10:16) Behold, <u>I send you forth as sheep in the midst of wolves: be ye therefore wise as serpents, and harmless as doves</u>.

(Matt 5:16) Let your light so shine before men, that they may see your good works, and glorify your Father which is in heaven.

(Phil 2:15) That ye may <u>be blameless and harmless</u>, the sons of God, without rebuke, in the midst of a crooked and perverse nation, among whom ye shine as lights in the world;

I am aware that the Bible makes it clear that if the person rejects Christ as his Savior, he will spend eternity in the lake of fire, and the unbeliever has no one to blame but himself. It is his own unbelief that sends him to hell. Notice the following passages.

(John 3:18) He that believeth on him is not condemned: but <u>he that believeth not is condemned already, because he hath not believed in the name of the only begotten Son of God.</u>

(John 3:36) He that believeth on the Son hath everlasting life: and <u>he that believeth not the Son shall not see life; but the wrath of God abideth on him.</u>

However, the believer does not want to stand before God, and God then reveals that he was actually a hinderance to people getting saved instead of a help to people getting saved.

Now let us turn our focus to the believer. We will start with a few passages of scripture.

(Gal 6:10) <u>As we have therefore opportunity, let us do good unto all *men*, especially unto them who are of the household of faith.</u>

(Matt 7:12) Therefore <u>all things whatsoever ye would that men should do to you, do ye even so to them: for this is the law and the prophets.</u>

The golden rule not only applies to how we treat the unbeliever, it also applies to how we treat the believer.

(Jas 5:19) <u>Brethren, if any of you do err</u> from the truth, and one convert him; (Jas 5:20) Let him know, that he which converteth the sinner from the error of his way shall save a soul from death, and shall hide a multitude of sins.

The above passage is referring to the backslidden believers and not unbelievers. Note the phrase, "Brethren, if any of you do err."

The believer must freely forgive and be sure not to bear grudges.

(Matt 6:14) For if ye forgive men their trespasses, your heavenly Father will also forgive you: (Matt 6:15) But if ye forgive not men their trespasses, neither will your Father forgive your trespasses.

(Matt 18:21) Then came Peter to him, and said, Lord, how oft shall my brother sin against me, and I forgive him? till seven times? (Matt 18:22) Jesus saith unto him, I say not unto thee, Until seven times: but, Until seventy times seven.

(Jas 5:9) <u>Grudge not one against another, brethren</u>, lest ye be condemned: behold, the judge standeth before the door.

We must also remember the second greatest command in the Bible. We must love our neighbor as ourselves. Many times, we are commanded to love one another. Note the following passages.

(Lev 19:18) Thou shalt not avenge, nor bear any grudge against the children of thy people, but <u>thou shalt love thy neighbour as thyself</u>: I *am* the LORD.

(Matt 22:39) And the second *is* like unto it, <u>Thou shalt love thy neighbour as thyself.</u>

(Mark 12:31) And the second *is* like, *namely* this, <u>Thou shalt love thy neighbour as thyself</u>. There is none other commandment greater than these.

(Luke 10:27) And he answering said, Thou shalt love the Lord thy God with all thy heart, and with all thy soul, and with all thy strength, and with all thy mind; and <u>thy neighbour as thyself.</u>

(Rom 13:9) For this, Thou shalt not commit adultery, Thou shalt not kill, Thou shalt not steal, Thou shalt not bear false witness, Thou shalt not covet; and if *there be* any other commandment, it is briefly comprehended in this saying, namely, <u>Thou shalt love thy neighbour as thyself</u>. (Rom 13:10) Love worketh no ill to his neighbour: therefore love *is* the fulfilling of the law.

(Gal 5:14) For all the law is fulfilled in one word, *even* in this; <u>Thou shalt love thy neighbour as thyself.</u>

(Jas 2:8) If ye fulfil the royal law according to the scripture, <u>Thou shalt love thy neighbour as thyself, ye do well:</u>

(1John 3:11) For this is the message that ye heard from the beginning, that <u>we should love one another.</u>

(1John 3:23) And this is his commandment, That we should believe on the name of his Son Jesus Christ, and <u>love one another</u>, as he gave us commandment.

(1John 4:7) Beloved, <u>let us love one another</u>: for love is of God; and every one that loveth is born of God, and knoweth God.

(1John 4:11) Beloved, if God so loved us, <u>we ought also to love one another</u>.

(1John 4:12) No man hath seen God at any time. <u>If we love one another, God dwelleth in us, and his love is perfected in us.</u>

We now live in a time when the impatient believer has a tendency to shoot their own wounded. There is an expression from the military that is called, "friendly fire." This expression comes from when a fellow soldier accidently shoots one of his own comrades. I am afraid that in the spiritual world, many a backslidden believer has been shot by the impatient believer and it is not exactly friendly fire. Unfortunately, we have the tendency to kick people while they are down.

(Gal 6:1) Brethren, if a man be overtaken in a fault, ye which are spiritual, restore such an one in the spirit of meekness; considering thyself, lest thou also be tempted.

11

Waiting with Patience

Successful waiting is definitely impossible without patience. According to G5281, successful waiting and patience are synonyms. So, <u>the person that is not waiting patiently is wasting time</u>. One of the mistakes that is made when we are put in an opportunity to have to wait is that we will choose to do nothing while we wait. <u>You are not designed to do nothing</u>. You must keep yourself busy doing other good things while you are put in a position to wait on other things. It is possible and necessary to stay busy and wait at the same time. This will help you to wait patiently. Allow me to illustrate.

You have a doctor's appointment and you know in advance that there will be a length of time in the waiting room. You are making a mistake if you do not have your New Testament with you to read or your prayer list to pray through while you wait. Always keep something with you that will keep you busy. I am not referring to pacifying the time. I am referring to using the waiting period of time wisely by doing something else that is constructive and productive for God.

In our modern world and with some modern technology there are things that now exist that will literally fuel impatience as a side-effect. They are not designed for that reason but because of the convenience they typically will produce impatience. I am not against technology, but we must be aware that some things that we are cutting corners and saving time on have a side-effect of impatience. Allow me to explain.

Most homes now are equipped with the microwave oven. Some food is now prepared quicker and served sooner than ever before. So, we do not have to wait as long for certain foods. That being said, this sets the stage for being impatient with the foods that do take longer to prepare.

Most homes have in their kitchens, different types of instant foods. Most have heard of instant grits or the complete cake mix that comes in a box. Again, the convenience and quickness of the food fuels impatience for the food that takes longer.

Fast food restaurants have the same effect. With the luxury of quickness and convenience comes the side effect of impatience when things are not so quick and convenient.

Like anything else that needs practice, when we are robbed of any opportunity to learn while waiting for something, we pass up the opportunity to practice staying busy while we wait for something else that is also important. We are not able to stay busy doing other good things while we wait, and we find ourselves looking for a neutral position and going into idleness. We must be aware of how dangerous idleness is. Notice the following passages.

(Prov 19:15) Slothfulness casteth into a deep sleep; and <u>an idle soul shall suffer hunger</u>.

(Prov 31:27) She looketh well to the ways of her household, and <u>eateth not the bread of idleness.</u>

(Eccl 10:18) By much slothfulness the building decayeth; and <u>through idleness of the hands the house droppeth through.</u>

(Ezek 16:49) Behold, this was the iniquity of thy sister Sodom, pride, fulness of bread, and <u>abundance of idleness</u> was in her and in her daughters, neither did she strengthen the hand of the poor and needy.

(1Tim 5:13) And withal <u>they learn *to be* idle</u>, wandering about from house to house; and <u>not only idle, but tattlers also and busybodies, speaking things which they ought not</u>.

Waiting is very unpopular due to the fact that we are typically very busy and impatient. God will put us in the position many times to wait and we will not have a choice, but we must not idle while we wait. We must stay busy.

Have good things planned to do to be on standby to fill in the gaps of the waiting periods.

Should I dare mention dieting? Everyone that needs to, will gladly lose weight, as long as it is quickly or even instantly done. The patience to lose weight methodically and gradually to avoid shocking your body's systems is almost a thing of the past and not heard of anymore. Because you have quick weight loss programs or surgically induced weight loss programs, good or bad, this has fueled the flames of impatience. We typically think that it is impossible to lose weight the normal way, because of our own impatience.

Allow me to use another illustration. I will start it out with some passages of scripture.

(Col 4:5) Walk in wisdom toward them that are without, <u>redeeming the time</u>.

(Eph 5:16) <u>Redeeming the time</u>, because the days are evil.

We are taught from the scripture to redeem the time that we have. Part of redeeming the time is to make full use of time and not waist time. As important as this is, if we are not careful, we will fuel the flames of impatience trying to save time and not to waste time. Allow me to illustrate.

You are driving your vehicle and you are running late for an appointment. You approach a traffic light. The light turns red, so unfortunately you have to stop, and you are delayed. Finally, the light turns green, so you are anxiously ready to go, but not as much as the person that is driving in front of you. They are moving but not nearly as fast as you think they should. So, with the tightening of your jaw, you sound the horn, thinking that it will save time. You manage to get around them and discover that it was someone you have been trying to witness to. Was it worth it?

You must fight for the balance to not waist time and be also patient. It is a dangerous thing to be put to waiting and have no patience to go with it. Again, stay busy while you wait.

It is interesting how many Bible verses mention waiting and patience in the same verse. Notice the following just to name a few.

(Ps 37:7) Rest in the LORD, and <u>wait patiently for him</u>: fret not thyself because of him who prospereth in his way, because of the man who bringeth wicked devices to pass.

(Ps 40:1) I <u>waited patiently for the LORD</u>; and he inclined unto me, and heard my cry.

(Rom 8:25) But if we hope for that we see not, <u>then do we with patience wait for it</u>.

(2Thess 3:5) And the Lord direct your hearts into the love of God, and into <u>the patient waiting for Christ.</u>

(Jas 5:7) <u>Be patient therefore, brethren, unto the coming of the Lord</u>. Behold, <u>the husbandman waiteth for the precious fruit of the earth, and hath long patience for it</u>, until he receive the early and latter rain.

(1Pet 3:20) Which sometime were disobedient, when once <u>the longsuffering of God waited</u> in the days of Noah, while the ark was a preparing, wherein few, that is, eight souls were saved by water.

In light of modern technology, I presently have four computers in my possession. Two towers and two laptops. I have a very powerful Bible program that has an amazing search engine on it. With this tool, I can scan in seconds the entire Bible of English, Greek, or Hebrew and even search for syllables as well as whole words and phrases of words. I have lived long enough to know that back in the old days this was totally unheard of. In the old days you searched through the Bible by reading word for word and book by book. This takes a lot of work and patience. I cannot imagine going back to the old days without the computer tools I have now. Yes, back then, it took a lot more time and much more patience to search through the Bible and find the things I needed.

So, remember, waiting without staying busy is wasting time. Perhaps you have heard the following statement. "Good things come to those that wait."

12

Patience in the Ministry

Before we deal with patience in the ministry, let's review the English synonyms and phrases for patience. They are as follows: Slow to Wrath; Longsuffering; Gentle; Moderation; Bear Long; Suffer Long; Patiently Endure; Endure; and Abide.

Now, can you imagine trying to operate in any kind of ministry without the above tools mentioned. Let's consider a pastor or a staff member with a bad temper. Can you imagine the damage that he will cause? Think about a pastor who just gets into the ministry and things start getting a little rough. Due to the absence of patience he will over-react and soon quit and go elsewhere or even get out of the ministry all together.

Allow me to inject in this place a summary resume of the ministry God has given me through the years. This author has been preaching, pastoring, or an associate pastor for over 45 years. I have always gone for the small churches through the years because I believe that this is what God had me to do. I have seen many situations where patience is absolutely priceless. This being said, please allow me to give you problems that I have experienced and seen in many churches and many ministries that I was in or ministries close to where I was located through the years that were brought on by impatience.

A pastor decides to lead his church to start a Christian school. He does so, not because he is led of God to do it. It was because it seemed that a lot of churches were doing it and he simply followed a fad instead of the Holy Spirit. He has unfortunately yielded to peer pressure from other churches or pastors, instead of patiently waiting on God for the okay. He charges on and almost destroys the church's finances and hence endangers the church's existence. Remember where God guides, God provides.

I have seen missionaries jump into a particular field or go to a particular location out of nothing but peer pressure instead of following God's leading. The missionary couple damages or even loses their own family trying to do something that God has not led them to do. You cannot expect God to help you do what he has not called you to do.

(1Thess 5:24) <u>Faithful *is* he that calleth you, who also will do *it*</u>.

I have seen many churches started and ministries started by churches that were a whim and were not started by the leading of the Holy Spirit. Allow me to name a few. Keep in mind, these ministries that I am about to name are wonderful ministries in themselves but if God has not led the pastor and church to do any of these ministries, they will harm the church instead of helping to edify and build the church. Again, allow me to name a few different ministries: The Bus Ministry; the Deaf Ministry; the Radio Ministry; and Christian Schools. If God does not lead the church to do any of these ministries, they will do more harm than good to the church.

I have seen many churches jump into debt to get something started and jump ahead of God and almost go under because they got so deep in debt. Some have actually closed and had to sell out due to being so deep in debt. They also destroy their own reputation by ruining their own credit. Notice the warning that God gives in the Bible.

(Prov 22:7) The rich ruleth over the poor, and <u>the borrower *is* servant to the lender</u>.

I have seen some churches compete with other churches on attendance and starting different ministries and still do more damage than good. <u>Remember what gets people to church, keeps people in church</u>. If the people go to church because they receive a prize or a promotion, they will expect to get a prize or a promotion every time they go.

If the prizes and promotions stop, they will typically stop going. If the person comes to church because they believe God wants them to go, they will have a better chance of continuing to go to church. Notice the following passages.

(1Cor 3:6) I have planted, Apollos watered; but <u>God gave the increase</u>. (1Cor 3:7) So then neither is he that planteth any thing, neither he that watereth; but <u>God that giveth the increase.</u>

Please study the following passage of scripture.

(2Cor 6:3) Giving no offence in any thing, that the ministry be not blamed: (2Cor 6:4) But in all things approving ourselves as the ministers of God, <u>in much patience</u>, in afflictions, in necessities, in distresses, (2Cor 6:5) In stripes, in imprisonments, in tumults, in labours, in watchings, in fastings; (2Cor 6:6) By pureness, by knowledge, <u>by longsuffering</u>, by kindness, by the Holy Ghost, by love unfeigned, (2Cor 6:7) By the word of truth, by the power of God, by the armour of righteousness on the right hand and on the left, (2Cor 6:8) By honour and dishonour, by evil report and good report: as deceivers, and yet true; (2Cor 6:9) As unknown, and yet well known; as dying, and, behold, we live; as chastened, and not killed; (2Cor 6:10) As sorrowful, yet alway rejoicing; as poor, yet making many rich; as having nothing, and yet possessing all things.

Patience is one of the Required
Qualifications of the Pastor

(1Tim 3:1) This *is* a true saying, If a man desire the office of a bishop, he desireth a good work. (1Tim 3:2) A bishop then must be blameless, the husband of one wife, vigilant, sober, of good behaviour, given to hospitality, apt to teach; (1Tim 3:3) <u>Not given to wine, no striker, not greedy of filthy lucre; but patient, not a brawler, not covetous;</u> (1Tim 3:4) One that ruleth well his own house, having his children in subjection with all gravity; (1Tim 3:5) (For if a man know not how to rule his own house, how shall he take care of the church of God?) (1Tim 3:6) Not a novice, lest being lifted up with pride he fall into the condemnation of the devil. (1Tim 3:7) Moreover he must have a good report of them which are without; lest he fall into reproach and the snare of the devil.

Notice in verse 3 God puts "patient" in the middle of 3 negatives on the left and 2 negatives on the right. On the left is "not given to wine, no striker, not greedy of filthy lucre and on the right is not a brawler, not covetous. The contrast is obvious. The patient one will not be addicted to wine and will be no striker and not greedy and not a brawler and not covetous.

Preaching in General

(2Tim 4:2) Preach the word; be instant in season, out of season; reprove, rebuke, <u>exhort with all longsuffering</u> and doctrine.

The preacher that preaches desiring to edify the believer and give the gospel to the unbeliever must reprove or convince and rebuke or charge and exhort or comfort with all longsuffering. Especially note the phrase, "all longsuffering." If he preaches without patience, he will do more damage than good. Also, for the truth's sake and detailing the gospel for the unbeliever and grounding the believer in the doctrine of the word of God, Bible teaching is just as important as preaching if not more so. The believers must be fed. They cannot be fed without doctrine and they cannot be fed without patience and the teacher cannot feed without patience. Notice the passages below on the emphasis God puts on feeding the believers.

(2Tim 2:2) And the things that thou hast heard of me among many witnesses, the same commit thou to faithful men, who shall be able to teach others also.

(John 21:15) So when they had dined, Jesus saith to Simon Peter, Simon, *son* of Jonas, lovest thou me more than these? He saith unto him, Yea, Lord; thou knowest that I love thee. He saith unto him, <u>Feed my lambs</u>. (John 21:16) He saith to him again the second time, Simon, *son* of Jonas, lovest thou me? He saith unto him, Yea, Lord; thou knowest that I love thee. He saith unto him, <u>Feed my sheep</u>. (John 21:17) He saith unto him the third time, Simon, *son* of Jonas, lovest thou me? Peter was grieved because he said unto him the third time, Lovest thou me? And he said unto him, Lord, thou knowest all things; thou knowest that I love thee. Jesus saith unto him, <u>Feed my sheep</u>.

(Acts 20:28) Take heed therefore unto yourselves, and to all the flock, over the which the Holy Ghost hath made you overseers, to <u>feed the church of God</u>, which he hath purchased with his own blood.

(1Pet 5:2) <u>Feed the flock of God</u> which is among you, taking the oversight *thereof,* not by constraint, but willingly; not for filthy lucre, but of a ready mind;

The Servant of the Lord

(2Tim 2:24) And the servant of the Lord must not strive; but be <u>gentle unto all men</u>, apt to teach, <u>patient</u>,

When the passage above mentions the phrase, "the servant of the Lord," it applies to any and every position in the ministry. For the believer to be a servant of the Lord, he must have a servant's heart. To have a servant's heart he must be patient. In order not to strive or fight or argue or fuss, he must be patient. In order to be gentle unto all men he must be patient. In order to teach others successfully he must be patient.

The Soulwinner

(Prov 11:30) The fruit of the righteous *is* a tree of life; and <u>he that winneth souls *is* wise.</u>

One of the very noticeable areas in the ministry that I have seen through the years that has a serious lack of patience in it is in the procedure of soulwinning itself.

By the grace of God, I have been soulwinning or visiting from door to door witnessing for over 45 years. I have gone with a partner and gone without a partner. Most of the time it is without a partner but of course I have always had the Holy Spirit as my silent partner.

There are many examples that I would like to share about the impatience that comes up in soulwinning. Allow me to list a few things miscellaneously.

The soulwinner can be so anxious to see someone saved that they almost try to get saved for them. They make the mistake of putting words in their mouth and getting too far ahead of the one being witnessed to. Impatience tries to trick or force or badger a person into getting saved. This is very wrong. No one gets saved that does not want to get saved. The impatient soulwinner even has a tendency to get ahead of the Holy Spirit.

The patient soulwinner must be clear and careful in giving the details of the gospel out to the unbeliever. Allow me to give you an example of how I start the procedure of witnessing.

After approaching the door and knocking on it, and when the person comes to the door, I introduce myself and then ask them, Do You go to church anywhere? Then I ask, "Do you have the assurance that you are going to heaven when you die? Depending on how they answer, I ask, "What exactly are you depending on to get you to heaven?" If the response is anything but Jesus and Him dying on the Cross to pay for my sins to save me from Hell, then I ask, "Could I take a few moments and show you from the Bible what God says to depend on to get you to heaven?"

Please understand in none of this is there a forced or badgered situation. If the individual at the door tells me no or not now or I do not have time, or they are not interested, I will courteously leave them a gospel track and go on to the next door.

If they say yes, I will thoroughly show them from the Bible how to be saved. When I am done, I will ask them if they want Jesus to be their personal Savior? If the answer is yes, then I will simply lead them in a prayer that they tell God in asking Christ to save their soul.

There is no rush and there is no race. You are not competing with anyone else.

Now, let's address the leading of the Holy Spirit and the convicting of the Holy Spirit in the matter of witnessing. We will start out with a few passages of scripture.

(John 6:44) <u>No man can come to me, except the Father which hath sent me draw him</u>: and I will raise him up at the last day.

(John 12:32) And <u>I, if I be lifted up from the earth, will draw all *men* unto me</u>.

The Soulwinner should be aware that the Holy Spirit convicts and draws the unbeliever as the believer clearly and carefully explains the Gospel to him. If the Soulwinner is in a rush and in some kind of foolish race, he runs the risk of not being clear with the explanation of the Gospel and the Holy Spirit has little to work with from the believer to get into the unbeliever's heart. Again, patience is extremely important in the witnessing process.

The believer without patience will be drawn to trying to win an argument instead of trying to win a soul. There is no time to argue or to be rude and even rash if you are going to witness with patience.

So, we can see that patience is not only required in the ministry, the ministry cannot function successfully without patience.

13

Patience with God

At first glance, it is hard to think of being impatient with the perfect and only God and that also can do no wrong and loves us unconditionally. Knowing that nothing is impossible with God. Just for a reminder, notice the following passages.

(Luke 1:37) For <u>with God nothing shall be impossible</u>.

(Jer 32:17) Ah Lord GOD! behold, thou hast made the heaven and the earth by thy great power and stretched out arm, *and* <u>there is nothing too hard for thee</u>:

(Jer 32:27) Behold, <u>I *am* the LORD, the God of all flesh: is there any thing too hard for me?</u>

After reading the above, the question that might come to mind is "So, what is the problem? How can the believer be impatient with God? One of the problems that typically occurs is that the impatient believer forgets that God is not on the same timetable with us. Notice the following.

(2Pet 3:8) But, beloved, be not ignorant of this one thing, that <u>one day *is* with the Lord as a thousand years, and a thousand years as one day.</u>

(Ps 90:4) <u>For a thousand years in thy sight *are but* as yesterday when it is past, and *as* a watch in the night.</u>

Have you ever been in a situation where you needed help from God, and you asked for help, but you also asked God to hurry? You are not alone. Notice the passages below where the psalmist asked God to help and to hurry.

(Ps 22:19) But be not thou far from me, O LORD: O my strength, <u>haste thee to help me.</u>

(Ps 38:22) <u>Make haste to help me</u>, O Lord my salvation.

(Ps 40:13) Be pleased, O LORD, to deliver me: O LORD, <u>make haste to help me.</u>

(Ps 70:1) <u>*Make haste*, O God, to deliver me; make haste to help me, O LORD.</u>

(Ps 70:5) But I *am* poor and needy: <u>make haste unto me, O God</u>: thou *art* my help and my deliverer; O LORD, <u>make no tarrying.</u>

(Ps 71:12) O God, <u>be not far from me: O my God, make haste for my help.</u>

It is worth pointing out that sometimes God acts on our behalf even before we know we need help. Notice the next passage.

(Ps 46:1) <u>God *is* our refuge and strength, a very present help in trouble</u>.

If we would just remind ourselves each day of some of God's amazing abilities and attributes, you think it would help us <u>not</u> to get impatient with God. Shall we review a few attributes of God again. God can do no wrong. God cannot make a mistake. God loves us with an unconditional love. God always wants what is best for us. God sees the beginning and the end of any situation.

There is more but in spite of those wonderful characteristics of God, we as believers have the tendency to get impatient with God. Notice the following passages of scripture.

(Ps 37:7) <u>Rest in the LORD, and wait patiently for him:</u> fret not thyself because of him who prospereth in his way, because of the man who bringeth wicked devices to pass.

(Ps 40:1) <u>I waited patiently for the LORD</u>; and he inclined unto me, and heard my cry.

There is a story in the Bible that illustrates the great danger that is involved when the believer is impatient with God and gets ahead of God. The damage to the individual's present and future is almost unmeasurable. This story involves Abraham, Abraham's servant, Eliezer, Sarah, and Sarah's maid, Hagar. Notice the following passages.

(Gen 15:1) After these things the word of the LORD came unto Abram in a vision, saying, Fear not, Abram: I *am* thy shield, *and* thy exceeding great reward. (Gen 15:2) And Abram said, Lord GOD, <u>what wilt thou give me, seeing I go childless, and the steward of my house *is* this Eliezer of Damascus?</u> (Gen 15:3) And <u>Abram said, Behold, to me thou hast given no seed: and, lo, one born in my house is mine heir</u>. (Gen 15:4) And, behold, the word of the LORD *came* unto him, saying, <u>This shall not be thine heir; but he that shall come forth out of thine own bowels shall be thine heir</u>.

(Gen 16:1) Now Sarai Abram's wife bare him no children: and she had an handmaid, an Egyptian, whose name was Hagar. (Gen 16:2) And Sarai said unto Abram, Behold now, the LORD hath restrained me from bearing: I pray thee, go in unto my maid; it may be that I may obtain children by her. And Abram hearkened to the voice of Sarai. (Gen 16:3) And <u>Sarai Abram's wife took Hagar her maid the Egyptian, after Abram had dwelt ten years in the land of Canaan, and gave her to her husband Abram to be his wife</u>. (Gen 16:4) And he went in unto Hagar, and she conceived: and when she saw that she had conceived, her mistress was despised in her eyes. (Gen 16:5) And Sarai said unto Abram, <u>My wrong be upon thee</u>: I have given my maid into thy bosom; and when she saw that she had conceived, I was despised in her eyes: the LORD judge between me and thee.

Abraham was 86 years old when Ishmael, the son of Hagar, was born unto Abraham. God had them wait 14 more years before Sarah had Isaac. Abraham was 100 years old upon Sarah having Isaac.

Oh, the damage we cause ourselves and the damage we cause in our world when we get ahead of God due to our impatience with God.

From the study in chapter 3, we see that successful waiting and patience go hand in hand. As has been said, it takes patience to wait and successful waiting is patience.

There are many benefits and blessings for waiting upon the Lord. Notice the following passages to name a few.

(Ps 37:9) For evildoers shall be cut off: but <u>those that wait upon the LORD, they shall inherit the earth.</u>

(Isa 40:31) But <u>they that wait upon the LORD shall renew *their* strength; they shall mount up with wings as eagles; they shall run, and not be weary; *and* they shall walk, and not faint.</u>

(Lam 3:25) <u>The LORD *is* good unto them that wait for him</u>, to the soul *that* seeketh him.

Somethings that Would Try to Get us Not to Wait on God and to Lose Our Patience with God

1) Fear

There are many things that would try to cause us <u>not</u> to wait upon the Lord. One of those things is fear. Fear causes God's people to panic and jump ahead of God. See the following.

(Ps 27:14) <u>Wait on the LORD: be of good courage, and he shall strengthen thine heart: wait, I say, on the LORD.</u>

(2Tim 1:7) For <u>God hath not given us the spirit of fear; but of power, and of love, and of a sound mind.</u>

2) The Lack of Trust

Another thing that tries to cause us <u>not</u> to wait upon God is a lack of trust in God. See the following.

(Ps 130:5) <u>I wait for the LORD, my soul doth wait, and in his word do I hope</u>.

(Isa 51:5) My righteousness *is* near; my salvation is gone forth, and mine arms shall judge the people; <u>the isles shall wait upon me, and on mine arm shall they trust</u>.

3) Vengeance

Another thing that tries to cause us to <u>not</u> wait upon God is personal vengeance. We get wronged in some way and have a tendency to take matters into our own hands. Vengeance belongs to God and not to the believer.

(Prov 20:22) <u>Say not thou, I will recompense evil; *but* wait on the LORD, and he shall save thee.</u>

(Deut 32:35) <u>To me *belongeth* vengeance, and recompence</u>; their foot shall slide in *due* time: for the day of their calamity *is* at hand, and the things that shall come upon them make haste.

(Ps 94:1) <u>O LORD God, to whom vengeance belongeth; O God, to whom vengeance belongeth, shew thyself</u>.

(Nah 1:2) <u>God *is* jealous, and the LORD revengeth; the LORD revengeth, and *is* furious; the LORD will take vengeance on his adversaries, and he reserveth *wrath* for his enemies.</u>

(Heb 10:30) For we know him that hath said, <u>Vengeance *belongeth* unto me, I will recompense, saith the Lord</u>. And again, The Lord shall judge his people.

(Rom 12:19) Dearly beloved, <u>avenge not yourselves, but *rather* give place unto wrath: for it is written, Vengeance *is* mine; I will repay, saith the Lord.</u>

4) Pride

Another thing that tries to cause us to <u>not</u> wait upon God is pride. We think we can handle some things ourselves and forget what Jesus said in the following passage.

(John 15:5) I am the vine, ye *are* the branches: He that abideth in me, and I in him, the same bringeth forth much fruit: for <u>without me ye can do nothing</u>.

(Eccl 7:8) Better *is* the end of a thing than the beginning thereof: *and* <u>the patient in spirit *is* better than the proud in spirit.</u>

    5)   The Unknown Future

Still another thing that tries to cause us <u>not</u> to wait upon God is the unknown future. As odd as it is, according to the Bible, the future is supposed to be unknown. God through the Bible has given us details about eternity future but will never tell us about tomorrow.

(Prov 27:1) Boast not thyself of to morrow; for <u>thou knowest not what a day may bring forth.</u>

(Jas 4:13) Go to now, ye that say, To day or to morrow we will go into such a city, and continue there a year, and buy and sell, and get gain: (Jas 4:14) Whereas <u>ye know not what *shall be* on the morrow</u>. For what *is* your life? It is even a vapour, that appeareth for a little time, and then vanisheth away. (Jas 4:15) For that ye *ought* to say, If the Lord will, we shall live, and do this, or that.

(Matt 6:33) But seek ye first the kingdom of God, and his righteousness; and all these things shall be added unto you. (Matt 6:34) <u>Take therefore no thought for the morrow: for the morrow shall take thought for</u>

the things of itself. Sufficient unto the day *is* the evil thereof.

(Rom 8:25) But if we hope for that we see not, *then* do we with patience wait for *it*.

6) Our Own Thoughts and Our Own Will and Our Own Plans

Sometimes the believer forgets that God's thoughts are not the same as our thoughts. Notice the following.

(Isa 55:8) For my thoughts *are* not your thoughts, neither *are* your ways my ways, saith the LORD. (Isa 55:9) For *as* the heavens are higher than the earth, so are my ways higher than your ways, and my thoughts than your thoughts.

Having said this, God has given the believer a manual that tells us all about God and how He thinks. From this Holy Book we can know that God will never lead us contrary to the Bible. God had it written, and God will not contradict the Bible.

The Bible is the sole and final authority for faith and practice. Now, notice the following passage.

(Phil 2:5) Let this mind be in you, which was also in Christ Jesus:

Getting the mind of Christ in us is made possible by studying your Bible. The Bible gives us the perfect profile of God in it and how God thinks and acts.

Where the believer gets in trouble is when the believer starts thinking his way instead of the way the Bible tells him to think. Notice the following passage.

(2Cor 10:5) Casting down imaginations, and every high thing that exalteth itself against the knowledge of God, and <u>bringing into captivity every thought to the obedience of Christ;</u>

The believer needs to realize how foolish we are when we get to thinking that we know better than God or that we can do things better than God.

I am sure there are more than these six things mentioned that can cause us to get impatient with God. However, these are some of the main things that can cause us to jump ahead of God and become impatient with God.

Now let's look at a partial list of some reasons on why we should wait patiently on God. Notice the following.

1) For Learning and Guidance

Psalm 25:3 Yea, let none that wait on thee be ashamed: let them be ashamed which transgress without cause. 4 <u>Shew me thy ways, O LORD; teach me thy paths</u>. 5 <u>Lead me in thy truth, and teach me</u>: for thou *art* the God of my salvation<u>; on thee do I wait all the day.</u>

2) For Courage and Strength

Psalm 27:14 Wait on the LORD: <u>be of good courage</u>, and <u>he shall strengthen thine heart: wait, I say, on the LORD.</u>

Isaiah 40:31 But <u>they that wait upon the LORD shall renew *their* strength</u>; they shall mount up with wings as eagles; they shall run, and not be weary; *and* they shall walk, and not faint.

3) For Answer to Prayer

Psalm 40:<u>1 I waited patiently for the LORD</u>; and <u>he inclined unto me</u>, and <u>heard my cry</u>.

4) For Provision

Psalm 104:27 <u>These wait all upon thee; that thou mayest give *them* their meat in due season.</u>

Psalm 145:15 <u>The eyes of all wait upon thee; and thou givest them their meat in due season.</u>

5) For Vengeance or Retaliation

Prov. 20:22 <u>Say not thou, I will recompense evil; *but* wait on the LORD, and he shall save thee.</u>

Psalm 94:1 <u>O LORD God, to whom vengeance belongeth; O God, to whom vengeance belongeth, shew thyself.</u>

6) For Defense

Psalm 33:20 <u>Our soul waiteth for the LORD: he</u> *is* <u>our help and our shield</u>.

Psalm 59:9 *Because of* his strength will <u>I wait upon thee: for God</u> *is* <u>my defence</u>.

7) For Getting us out of Problems and Difficulties

Lamentations 3:25-26 <u>The LORD</u> *is* <u>good unto them that wait for him, to the soul</u> *that* <u>seeketh him.</u> *It is* <u>good that</u> *a man* <u>should both hope and quietly wait for the salvation of the LORD.</u>

14

Episodes of Those in the Bible with Patience and Those without Patience

(Jas 5:10) Take, my brethren, the prophets, who have spoken in the name of the Lord, for an <u>example of suffering affliction, and of patience</u>.

Job with Patience

It might be worth noting that in the book of Job itself, there is not one mention of the word "patience" in the entire 42 chapters. However, patience is illustrated throughout the whole book of Job.

It is important to say up front that what Job went through was not chastisement for sin. It was a test from God. Notice the statement that God said to Satan.

(Job 2:3) And the LORD said unto Satan, Hast thou considered my servant Job, that *there is* none like him in the earth, a perfect and an upright man, one that feareth God, and escheweth evil? and still he holdeth fast his integrity, <u>although thou movedst me against him, to destroy him without cause.</u>

"Without cause" means that the things that God put Job through were a test from God and not chastisement for his sin. Job was not living in some kind of sin. Job's friends thought otherwise and accused Job of living in some kind of horrible sin. That seems to be the trend among believers is to jump to conclusion over other believers that are going through hard times that they are backslidden on God and are being chastised by God.

Examples of Some Accusations from Job's Friends to Job

(Job 4:7) Remember, I pray thee, <u>who *ever* perished, being innocent</u>? or where were the righteous cut off? (Job 4:8) Even as I have seen, <u>they that plow iniquity, and sow wickedness, reap the same.</u>

(Job 4:17) Shall mortal man be more just than God? shall a man be more pure than his maker?

(Job 8:4) <u>If thy children have sinned against him, and he have cast them away for their transgression;</u>

(Job 22:5) <u>*Is* not thy wickedness great</u>? <u>and thine iniquities</u> <u>infinite</u>? (Job 22:6) For thou hast taken a pledge from thy brother for nought, and stripped the naked of their clothing. (Job 22:7) Thou hast not given water to the weary to drink, and thou hast withholden bread from the hungry.

(Job 34:31) Surely it is meet to be said unto God, <u>I have</u> <u>borne *chastisement*, I will not offend *any more*</u>:

(Job 34:37) For <u>he addeth rebellion unto his sin</u>, he clappeth *his hands* among us, and multiplieth his words against God.

Now, to briefly summarize the test that God put Job through, notice the following passages.

(Job 1:12) And <u>the LORD said unto Satan, Behold, all</u> <u>that he hath *is* in thy power; only upon himself put not</u> <u>forth thine hand.</u> So Satan went forth from the presence of the LORD. (Job 1:13) And there was a day when his sons and his daughters *were* eating and drinking wine in their eldest brother's house: (Job 1:14) And there came a messenger unto Job, and said, The oxen were plowing, and the asses feeding beside them: (Job 1:15) And the Sabeans fell *upon them*, and took them away; yea<u>, they</u> <u>have slain the servants with the edge of the sword</u>; and I only am escaped alone to tell thee. (Job 1:16) While he *was* yet speaking, there came also another, and said, The fire of God is fallen from heaven, <u>and hath burned up</u>

the sheep, and the servants, and consumed them; and I only am escaped alone to tell thee. (Job 1:17) While he *was* yet speaking, there came also another, and said, The Chaldeans made out three bands, and fell upon the camels, and have carried them away, yea, and slain the servants with the edge of the sword; and I only am escaped alone to tell thee. (Job 1:18) While he *was* yet speaking, there came also another, and said, Thy sons and thy daughters *were* eating and drinking wine in their eldest brother's house: (Job 1:19) And, behold, there came a great wind from the wilderness, and smote the four corners of the house, and it fell upon the young men, and they are dead; and I only am escaped alone to tell thee.

Job loses his servants, his livestock, and all ten of his children at one time and there is still more. Notice the following.

(Job 2:6) And the LORD said unto Satan, Behold, he *is* in thine hand; but save his life. (Job 2:7) So went Satan forth from the presence of the LORD, and smote Job with sore boils from the sole of his foot unto his crown.

(Job 7:5) My flesh is clothed with worms and clods of dust; my skin is broken, and become loathsome.

Job loses his health but there is still more.

(Job 2:9) Then said his wife unto him, Dost thou still retain thine integrity? curse God, and die.

Job loses his wife's loyalty to him and God but there is still more.

(Job 7:14) Then thou scarest me with dreams, and terrifiest me through visions:

Job loses his ability to rest and sleep because of nightmares and is visited by three friends that accuse Job of living in sin. The friends thought Job was being chastised and judged by God for his sin when instead Job was being tested by God. Yet, there is still more.

(Job 19:14) My kinsfolk have failed, and my familiar friends have forgotten me. (Job 19:15) They that dwell in mine house, and my maids, count me for a stranger: I am an alien in their sight. (Job 19:16) I called my servant, and he gave *me* no answer; I intreated him with my mouth. (Job 19:17) My breath is strange to my wife, though I intreated for the children's *sake* of mine own body. (Job 19:18) Yea, young children despised me; I arose, and they spake against me. (Job 19:19) All my inward friends abhorred me: and they whom I loved are turned against me. (Job 19:20) My bone cleaveth to my skin and to my flesh, and I am escaped with the skin of my teeth.

Those that knew Job shunned him. Job's kinsfolk, his familiar friends, even those that dwell in Job's own house shunned Job. Even Job's wife shunned Job. Young children despised Job and Job's inward friends abhorred

Job. The people that Job loved turned against him. Also, Job physically became skin and bones.

So, how did Job get through all of this and come out with double of that which he had before. The statements that Job will tell us through the trials reveals what is going on inside of Job's heart and mind during the trials. Notice the following.

Job believed everything is for God's to take or to give.

Job 1:21 And said, Naked came I out of my mother's womb, and naked shall I return thither: <u>the LORD gave, and the LORD hath taken away; blessed be the name of the LORD</u>.

Job had the right perspective of Heaven.

Job 3:17 *There* the wicked cease *from* troubling; and <u>there</u> the weary be at rest. 18 *There* the prisoners rest together; they hear not the voice of the oppressor. 19 The small and great are <u>there</u>; and the servant *is* free from his master.

Job had unwavering trust in God.

Job 13:15 <u>Though he slay me, yet will I trust in him</u>: but I will maintain mine own ways before him.

Job had assurance of his Salvation.

Job 19:25 For <u>I know *that* my redeemer liveth</u>, and *that* he shall stand at the latter *day* upon the earth: 26 And *though* after my skin *worms* destroy this *body*, yet <u>in my flesh shall I see God</u>: 27 <u>Whom I shall see for myself</u>, and <u>mine eyes shall behold</u>, and not another; *though* my reins be consumed within me.

Job valued God's word.

Job 23:12 Neither have I gone back from the commandment of his lips; <u>I have esteemed the words of his mouth more than my necessary *food*.</u>

Job was determined to do right.

Job 27:4 <u>My lips shall not speak wickedness, nor my tongue utter deceit</u>. Job 27:5 God forbid that I should justify you: <u>till I die I will not remove mine integrity from me</u>.

Job 31:1 <u>I made a covenant with mine eyes; why then should I think upon a maid?</u>

In the previous statements that Job made we can see the roots of Job's fruit of patience. With all this said under the inspiration of the Holy Spirit, James says that <u>Job had patience</u> to get him through all the tests and trials. See the following passage.

(Jas 5:11) Behold, we count them happy which endure. <u>Ye have heard of the patience of Job</u>, and have seen the end of the Lord; that the Lord is very pitiful, and of tender mercy.

Job was a very patient man.

Joseph with Patience

Allow me to share some of the trials that Joseph went through and much of it was from his own family. Notice the following passages.

(Gen 37:3) Now <u>Israel loved Joseph more than all his children</u>, because he *was* the son of his old age: and he made him a coat of *many* colours. (Gen 37:4) And when <u>his brethren saw that their father loved him more than all his brethren, they hated him</u>, and could not speak peaceably unto him.

Note: Israel put Joseph in a very difficult position because he favored Joseph over the other sons and the other sons knew it and hated Joseph for it when it was not Joseph's fault.

(Gen 37:5) And <u>Joseph dreamed a dream, and he told *it* his brethren: and they hated him yet the more</u>. (Gen 37:6) And he said unto them, Hear, I pray you, this dream which I have dreamed: (Gen 37:7) For, behold, we *were* binding sheaves in the field, and, lo, my sheaf arose, and also stood upright; and, behold, your sheaves stood round about, and made obeisance to my sheaf. (Gen 37:8) And his brethren said to him, Shalt thou indeed reign over us? or shalt thou indeed have dominion over us? And they hated him yet the more for his dreams, and for his words. (Gen 37:9) And he dreamed yet another dream, and told it his brethren, and said, Behold, I have dreamed a dream more; and, behold, the sun and the moon and the eleven stars made obeisance to me. (Gen 37:10) And he told *it* to his father, and to his brethren: and his father rebuked him, and said unto him, What *is* this dream that thou hast dreamed? Shall I and thy mother and thy brethren indeed come to bow down ourselves to thee to the earth? (Gen 37:11) And his brethren envied him; but his father observed the saying.

Note: Joseph's dreams were not fabricated or made up. God sent those dreams to Joseph to give Joseph heads up on what would later come, and Joseph was hated by his brothers for the dreams.

(Gen 37:18) And when they saw him afar off, even before he came near unto them, they conspired against him to slay him. (Gen 37:19) And they said one to another, Behold, this dreamer cometh. (Gen 37:20) <u>Come now therefore, and let us slay him</u>, and cast him into some pit, and we will say, Some evil beast hath devoured him: and we shall see what will become of his dreams.

Note: Joseph is now hated by his own brothers to the point that some of them wanted to kill Joseph.

(Gen 37:36) And the Midianites sold him into Egypt unto Potiphar, an officer of Pharaoh's, *and* captain of the guard.

Note: Joseph is sold by his own brothers into slavery.

(Gen 39:7) And it came to pass after these things, that his master's wife cast her eyes upon Joseph; and she said, Lie with me. (Gen 39:8) But he refused, and said unto his master's wife, Behold, my master wotteth not what *is* with me in the house, and he hath committed all that he hath to my hand; (Gen 39:9) *There is* none greater in this house than I; neither hath he kept back any thing from me but thee, because thou *art* his wife: how then can I do this great wickedness, and sin against God? (Gen 39:10) And it came to pass, as she spake to Joseph day by day, that he hearkened not unto her, to lie by her, *or* to be with her. (Gen 39:11) And it came to pass about this time, that *Joseph* went into the house to do his business; and *there was* none of the men of the house there within. (Gen 39:12) And she caught him by his garment, saying, Lie with me: and he left his garment in her hand, and fled, and got him out. (Gen 39:13) And it came to pass, when she saw that he had left his garment in her hand, and was fled forth, (Gen 39:14) That she called unto the men of her house, and spake unto them, saying, See, he hath brought in an Hebrew unto us to mock us; he came in unto me to lie with me, and I cried with a loud voice: (Gen 39:15) And it came to pass, when he heard that I lifted up my voice and cried, that he left his garment with me, and fled, and got him out. (Gen 39:16) And she laid up his garment by her, until his lord came home. (Gen 39:17) And she spake unto him according to these words, saying, The Hebrew servant, which thou hast brought unto us, came in unto me to mock me: (Gen 39:18) And it came to pass, as I lifted up my voice and cried, that he left his garment with me, and fled out. (Gen 39:19) And it came to pass, when his master heard the words of his wife, which she spake unto him, saying, After this manner did thy servant to me; that his wrath was kindled. (Gen 39:20) And Joseph's master took him, and put him into the prison, a place where the king's prisoners *were* bound: and he was there in the prison.

Note: Joseph is set up and framed by his master's wife and thrown into prison.

(Gen 40:23) Yet did not the chief butler remember Joseph, but forgat him.

(Gen 41:1) And it came to pass at the end of <u>two full years</u>, that Pharaoh dreamed: and, behold, he stood by the river.

Note: Joseph was forgotten in prison for two years. With all that Joseph went through, Joseph did not get bitter with God. Joseph did not rebel against God but trusted God and patiently and successfully went through each test and trial and passed with flying colors and became second in command over Egypt and God used Joseph to save the entire nation of Israel.

One of the things that came up during Joseph's life of trials is that it was pointed out in the Scriptures that God was always with Joseph. Notice the following.

(Gen 39:2) And <u>the LORD was with Joseph</u>, and he was a prosperous man; and he was in the house of his master the Egyptian.

(Gen 39:3) And his master saw that <u>the LORD *was* with him</u>, and that the LORD made all that he did to prosper in his hand.

(Gen 39:21) But <u>the LORD was with Joseph</u>, and shewed him mercy, and gave him favour in the sight of the keeper of the prison.

(Gen 39:23) The keeper of the prison looked not to any thing *that was* under his hand; because <u>the LORD was with him</u>, and *that* which he did, the LORD made *it* to prosper.

Patience will help you focus on the reality that God has promised never to leave us nor forsake us.

(Heb 13:5) *Let your* conversation *be* without covetousness; *and be* content with such things as ye have: for he hath said, <u>I will never leave thee, nor forsake thee</u>.

<u>*Joseph was a very patient man*</u>.

Three of the Seven Churches in the Book of Revelation Commended for Patience

Now let us consider three of the seven churches mentioned in the book of Revelation that are commended for their patience. Now, you have to realize that of all the things that God commended the churches for, patience was brought up by God with a very high commendation. This reveals the value that God sees in patience and the desire that God wants to see patience in all the believers in all the churches.

The Church #1 of Ephesus

(Rev 2:2) I know thy works, and thy labour, and <u>thy patience</u>, and how thou canst not bear them which are evil: and thou hast tried them which say they are apostles, and are not, and hast found them liars:

(Rev 2:3) And hast borne, and <u>hast patience</u>, and for my name's sake hast laboured, and hast not fainted.

> *Note: Please do not overlook the fact that the Church of Ephesus was commended by God for their patience two times.*

The Church #3 in Thyatira

(Rev 2:19) I know thy works, and charity, and service, and faith, and <u>thy patience</u>, and thy works; and the last to be more than the first.

The Church #5 in Philadelphia

(Rev 3:10) Because thou hast kept the word of my patience, I also will keep thee from the hour of temptation, which shall come upon all the world, to try them that dwell upon the earth.

The Saints in General

(Rev 13:10) He that leadeth into captivity shall go into captivity: he that killeth with the sword must be killed with the sword. Here is the patience and the faith of the saints.

Due to the phrase in the above passage which states, "here is the patience and faith of the saints," we must understand the context. We see that God has commanded for those that kill with the sword must be killed by the sword. Another phrase for this is "capital punishment." This truth is taught from Genesis to Revelation. Notice the next passage.

(Gen 9:6) Whoso sheddeth man's blood, by man shall his blood be shed: for in the image of God made he man.

Please see this author's book, "What the Bible says about Death." In chapter 4, this author goes into more detail on capital punishment.

So, the patience and faith of the saints is that the believer needs to know that no one anywhere gets away with anything. To summarize this, notice the following.

The person that trusts Christ as his Savior is saved from going to Hell when he dies. Now if the believer sins against God after he has trusted Christ, God promises out of love to chastise him. So, the believer will be chastised for his sin in this life.

(Heb 12:5) And ye have forgotten the exhortation which speaketh unto you as unto children, My son, despise not thou the chastening of the Lord, nor faint when thou art rebuked of him: (Heb 12:6) For whom the Lord loveth he chasteneth, and scourgeth every son whom he receiveth. (Heb 12:7) If ye endure chastening, God dealeth with you as with sons; for what son is he whom the father chasteneth not? (Heb 12:8) But if ye be without chastisement, whereof all are partakers, then are ye bastards, and not sons. (Heb 12:9) Furthermore we have had fathers of our flesh which corrected *us*, and we gave *them* reverence: shall we not much rather be in subjection unto the Father of spirits, and live? (Heb 12:10) For they verily for a few days chastened *us* after their own pleasure; but he for *our* profit, that *we* might be partakers of his holiness. (Heb 12:11) Now no chastening for the present seemeth to be joyous, but grievous: nevertheless afterward it yieldeth the peaceable fruit of righteousness unto them which are exercised thereby.

If the person dies without trusting Christ as his Savior, he will answer for every sin that he has ever done at the "White Throne Judgment" and then will be placed into his part of the lake of fire.

(Rev 20:11) And I saw a great white throne, and him that sat on it, from whose face the earth and the heaven fled away; and there was found no place for them. (Rev 20:12) And I saw the dead, small and great, stand before God; and the books were opened: and another book was opened, which is *the book* of life: and the dead were judged out of those things which were written in the books, according to their works. (Rev 20:13) And the sea gave up the dead which were in it; and death and hell delivered up the dead which were in them: and they were judged every man according to their works. (Rev 20:14) And death and hell were cast into the lake of fire. This is the second death. (Rev 20:15) And whosoever was not found written in the book of life was cast into the lake of fire.

The believer faces what he has done in this life as a believer and will receive rewards or no rewards at the "Judgment Seat of Christ."

(Rom 14:10) But why dost thou judge thy brother? or why dost thou set at nought thy brother? for we shall all stand before the judgment seat of Christ. (Rom 14:11) For it is written, *As* I live, saith the Lord, every knee shall bow to me, and every tongue shall confess to God. (Rom 14:12) So then every one of us shall give account of himself to God.

In this life, both the believer and the unbeliever will face the law of sowing and reaping, and it cannot be avoided.

(Gal 6:7) Be not deceived; God is not mocked: for whatsoever a man soweth, that shall he also reap.

So, you see, no one anywhere gets away with anything. That being said, this should help strengthen the patience that the believer will have toward all humanity and God. We will all one way or another have to answer to God. If the believer is frustrated by thinking someone has gotten away with something that is wrong, this frustration will only strengthen impatience in his life. Repeating, no one gets away with anything.

(Rev 14:9) And the third angel followed them, saying with a loud voice, If any man worship the beast and his image, and receive *his* mark in his forehead, or in his hand, (Rev 14:10) <u>The same shall drink of the wine of the wrath of God</u>, which is poured out without mixture into the cup of his indignation; and <u>he shall be tormented with fire and brimstone in the presence of the holy angels, and in the presence of the Lamb</u>: (Rev 14:11) And <u>the smoke of their torment ascendeth up for ever and ever: and they have no rest day nor night</u>, who worship the beast and his image, and whosoever receiveth the mark of his name. (Rev 14:12) <u>Here is the patience of the saints</u>: here are they that keep the commandments of God, and the faith of Jesus.

From the above passages, the phrase, "here is the patience of the saints," we see that the phrase is directly related to the unbeliever who will one day be placed into the lake of fire. The point is that the believer needs to stay conscious of the unbeliever's condemnation and do whatever he can to get the gospel to the unbeliever so that he can get saved and go to heaven instead of hell. The patience comes in because of knowing the horror of where they might spend eternity. The believer needs to be as patient as possible with the unbeliever. The believer does not want to be one that would hinder the unbeliever from getting saved due to his own impatience and careless treatment of the unbeliever.

Some Believers in the Bible that Displayed Impatience

Moses in an Episode without Patience

(Num 20:7) And the LORD spake unto Moses, saying, (Num 20:8) Take the rod, and gather thou the assembly together, thou, and Aaron thy brother, and <u>speak ye unto the rock</u> before their eyes; and it shall give forth his water, and thou shalt bring forth to them water out of the rock: so thou shalt give the congregation and their beasts drink. (Num 20:9) And Moses took the rod from before the LORD, as he commanded him. (Num 20:10) And Moses and Aaron gathered the congregation together before the rock, and he said unto them, <u>Hear now, ye rebels; must we fetch you water out of this rock</u>? (Num 20:11) And <u>Moses lifted up his hand, and with his rod he smote the rock twice</u>: and the water came out abundantly, and the congregation drank, and their beasts *also*. (Num 20:12)

And the LORD spake unto Moses and Aaron, Because ye believed me not, to sanctify me in the eyes of the children of Israel, therefore <u>ye shall not bring this congregation into the land which I have given them.</u>

In this heart-breaking episode this is the second time that there is a situation with receiving water from a rock mentioned in detail.

The first was in Exodus 17:5-6. In the first episode God specifically told Moses to strike the rock only once. Since the rock was a type of Christ (I Cor 10:4) the striking of the rock was picturing the crucifixion.

(Exod 17:5) And the LORD said unto Moses, Go on before the people, and take with thee of the elders of Israel; and thy rod, wherewith thou smotest the river, take in thine hand, and go. (Exod 17:6) Behold, I will stand before thee there upon the rock in Horeb; and <u>thou shalt smite the rock</u>, and there shall come water out of it, that the people may drink. And Moses did so in the sight of the elders of Israel.

(1Cor 10:4) And did all drink the same spiritual drink: for they drank of that spiritual Rock that followed them: and <u>that Rock was Christ.</u>

In the second episode God specifically tells Moses to speak to the rock. Moses with a display of impatience strikes the rock twice. The reason God told Moses to speak to the rock this time was because the crucifixion had already been illustrated earlier in the first episode. Now, Moses distorts the picture of the crucifixion by striking the rock twice and also includes himself for credit in fetching the water with the pronoun, we.

(Ps 106:32) They angered *him* also at the waters of strife, so that it went ill with Moses for their sakes: (Ps 106:33) Because they provoked his spirit, so that <u>he spake unadvisedly with his lips.</u>

Moses' impatience moved God to stop Moses from going into the promise land.

Saul in an Episode without Patience

(1Sam 13:6) When the men of Israel saw that they were in a strait, (for the people were distressed,) then the people did hide themselves in caves, and in thickets, and in rocks, and in high places, and in pits. (1Sam 13:7) And *some of* the Hebrews went over Jordan to the land of Gad and Gilead. As for Saul, he *was* yet in Gilgal, and all the people followed him trembling. (1Sam 13:8) And he tarried seven days, according to the set time that Samuel *had appointed*: but Samuel came not to Gilgal; and the people were scattered from him. (1Sam 13:9) And <u>Saul said, Bring hither a burnt offering to me, and peace offerings. And he offered the burnt offering.</u> (1Sam 13:10) And it came to pass, that as soon as he had made an end of offering the burnt offering, behold, Samuel came; and Saul went out to meet him, that he might salute him. (1Sam 13:11)

And <u>Samuel said, What hast thou done</u>? And Saul said, Because I saw that the people were scattered from me, and *that* <u>thou camest not within the days appointed</u>, and *that* the Philistines gathered themselves together at Michmash;

> *Note: Samuel did come within the days appointed because he was there when Saul foolishly took it upon himself and offered a sacrifice.*

(1Sam 13:12) Therefore said I, The Philistines will come down now upon me to Gilgal, and I have not made supplication unto the LORD: <u>I forced myself therefore, and offered a burnt offering.</u> (1Sam 13:13) And <u>Samuel said to Saul, Thou hast done foolishly: thou hast not kept the commandment of the LORD thy God, which he commanded thee: for now would the LORD have established thy kingdom upon Israel for ever.</u> (1Sam 13:14) <u>But now thy kingdom shall not continue: the LORD hath sought him a man after his own heart, and the LORD hath commanded him *to be* captain over his people, because thou hast not kept *that* which the LORD commanded thee.</u>

Because of Saul's impatience, he jumped into doing something that was not his to do. Because of Saul's impatience, God would remove the kingdom of Israel from him and he would no longer be king.

15

The Fruit of Patience and Patience as a Fruit

One of the characteristics of fruit that we must always keep in mind is that there is no such thing as instant fruit. Developing fruit unfortunately takes time and effort and patience.

Perhaps you have heard the story of "Jack and the Bean Stalk." The stalk shot up overnight. As you well know that was not a true story. How wonderful it would be if we as believers could instantly bear fruit. Remember that outside of salvation, very few things are instant. I have heard it said, "That which grows up overnight dies overnight." See the following passage to illustrate this point.

(Jonah 4:6) And <u>the LORD God prepared a gourd, and made *it* to come up over Jonah, that it might be a shadow over his head, to deliver him from his grief</u>. So Jonah was exceeding glad of the gourd. (Jonah 4:7) But <u>God prepared a worm when the morning rose</u> <u>the next day, and it smote the gourd that it withered</u>.

(Jonah 4:10) Then said the LORD, Thou hast had pity on the gourd, for the which thou hast not laboured, neither madest it grow; <u>which came up in a night, and perished in a night:</u>

Remember the things that are instant have a tendency to have a side effect of creating impatience in the one doing the receiving.

You will discover from the passages below that not only does patience help you bear fruit, but you will see also that patience actually is part of the fruit of the Spirit that God will help you bear.

(Gal 5:22) But the <u>fruit of the Spirit</u> is love, joy, peace, <u>longsuffering</u>, gentleness, goodness, faith, (Gal 5:23) Meekness, temperance: against such there is no law.

(Col 1:10) That ye might walk worthy of the Lord unto all pleasing, <u>being fruitful</u> in every good work, and increasing in the knowledge of God; (Col 1:11) Strengthened with all might, according to his glorious power, unto <u>all patience and longsuffering</u> with joyfulness;

(Jas 5:7) <u>Be patient</u> therefore, brethren, unto the coming of the Lord. Behold, <u>the husbandman waiteth for the precious fruit of the earth, and hath long patience for it</u>, until he receive the early and latter rain.

Since patience is a fruit and it takes patience to bear fruit, we need to be more conscience of the way this fruit develops in the believer. Again, it is not instant. Salvation is instant. Bearing fruit is not instant. Notice the pattern of growth mentioned in the following passage.

(Isa 37:31) And the remnant that is escaped of the house of Judah shall again <u>take root downward, and bear fruit upward:</u>

If we as believers do not take root downward, we will not bear fruit upward. The believer must realize that they must get themselves grounded in the Bible as soon as possible. If the tree has no root, it has no chance to survive and live long enough to bear fruit. The believer must as soon as possible yield to Jesus being Lord of their life after they have trusted Christ as their Savior. The believer must as soon as possible turn from any and all sin they are guilty of after they have trusted Christ as their Savior. Notice the following passage.

(Matt 13:5) Some fell upon stony places, where they had not much earth: and forthwith they sprung up, because they had no deepness of earth: (Matt 13:6) And when the sun was up, they were scorched; and <u>because they had no root, they withered away</u>.

Remember the divine order that God gives us of our development as believers is in the following passage.

(2Pet 1:5) And beside this, giving all diligence, <u>add to your faith virtue; and to virtue knowledge;</u> (2Pet 1:6) <u>And to knowledge temperance; and to temperance patience; and to patience godliness;</u> (2Pet 1:7) <u>And to godliness brotherly kindness; and to brotherly kindness charity.</u>

Your roots are your faith in the Word of God. Your roots are your stability.

(Isa 33:6) And <u>wisdom and knowledge shall be the stability of thy times, *and* strength of salvation:</u> the fear of the LORD *is* his treasure.

(Prov 12:3) A man shall not be established by wickedness: but <u>the root of the righteous shall not be moved.</u>

(Prov 12:12) The wicked desireth the net of evil *men*: but <u>the root of the righteous yieldeth *fruit.*</u>

Your faith must grow, and learning is directly connected with growing. If you are not learning you are not growing. Study the following passages.

(Rom 10:17) So then <u>faith *cometh* by hearing, and hearing by the word of God.</u>

(2Thess 1:3) We are bound to thank God always for you, brethren, as it is meet, because that <u>your faith groweth exceedingly</u>, and the charity of every one of you all toward each other aboundeth;

(2Pet 3:18) But <u>grow in grace, and *in* the knowledge of our Lord and Saviour Jesus Christ</u>. To him *be* glory both now and for ever. Amen.

The source of wisdom and knowledge is the Word of God. You must learn the Word of God to gain your stability because knowing the wisdom and knowledge from the Bible establishes your roots. Wisdom and knowledge are the strength of your salvation because even though God promises you heaven because you have trusted Christ as your Savior, the believer can doubt his salvation or even lose the joy of his salvation. However, the believer cannot lose his salvation. The strength of your salvation is the assurance and joy of your salvation. The believer that has lost the joy of his salvation or doubts his salvation has also lost the strength of his salvation in this life even though he is still promised heaven. With that he damages any development of spiritual fruit in his life.

(Neh 8:10) Then he said unto them, Go your way, eat the fat, and drink the sweet, and send portions unto them for whom nothing is prepared: for *this* day *is* holy unto our Lord: neither be ye sorry; for <u>the joy of the LORD is your strength</u>.

The spiritually healthy believer can expect to bear fruit all of his life, but he will bear fruit none of his life if he has no patience.

(Ps 92:14) <u>They shall still bring forth fruit in old age</u>; they shall be fat and flourishing;

(Job 14:8) <u>Though the root thereof wax old in the earth, and the stock thereof die in the ground;</u> (Job 14:9) <u>*Yet* through the scent of water it will bud, and bring forth boughs like a plant.</u>

(Jer 17:8) For <u>he shall be as a tree planted by the waters, and *that* spreadeth out her roots by the river</u>, and shall not see when heat cometh, but her leaf shall be green; and shall not be careful in the year of drought, <u>neither shall cease from yielding fruit.</u>

The water that the root seeks is the word of God. Notice the following.

(Eph 5:26) That he might sanctify and cleanse it with the <u>washing of water by the word,</u>

Without patience there can be no fruit.

(Luke 8:15) But that on the good ground are they, which in an honest and good heart, having heard the word, keep *it*, and <u>bring forth fruit with patience</u>.

(Eph 3:17) <u>That Christ may dwell in your hearts by faith; that ye, being rooted and grounded in love,</u>

16

Patience versus the Promises of God

One of the things that believers need to be aware of as soon as possible is that typically there is a different span of time between believing and meeting the conditions of God's promises and receiving God's promises. Typically, in that space is where the believer's faith is tested. You will notice that many times the believer gets answers to his or her prayers but rarely are they instant. Notice the following passage for an example. Paul asked God three times to remove his thorn in the flesh.

(2Cor 12:7) And lest I should be exalted above measure through the abundance of the revelations, there was given to me a thorn in the flesh, the messenger of Satan to buffet me, lest I should be exalted above measure. (2Cor 12:8) <u>For this thing I besought the Lord thrice, that it might depart from me</u>. (2Cor 12:9) And he said unto me, My grace is sufficient for thee: for my strength is made perfect in weakness. Most gladly therefore will I rather glory in my infirmities, that the power of Christ may rest upon me.

The one thing that is instant is salvation. The very moment the Hell-deserving sinner puts his faith in Jesus and appeals for Jesus to save his soul, believing that He was crucified on the cross, was buried, and resurrected for the salvation of his soul, he is instantly saved and promised heaven.

On other matters for the believer, most things that come from God are rarely instant. This is where patience comes in. Notice the following passages.

(Heb 6:12) That ye be not slothful, but followers of them who <u>through faith and patience inherit the promises.</u>

(Heb 6:15) And so, <u>after he had patiently endured, he obtained the promise</u>.

(Heb 10:36) For <u>ye have need of patience, that, after ye have done the will of God, ye might receive the promise.</u>

When the condition and requirement for a promise is met by the believer, the believer needs to be aware of the delay that sometimes comes when receiving the promise and the delay lasts as long as God sees fit. The believer will have a tendency to doubt himself or God when the believer does not receive the promise instantly. The believer might even get frustrated and give up. It will reveal whether or not the believer is operating on a whim or is operating with genuine faith. Is the believer using God as an experiment or is he genuinely trusting and waiting on God?

The space between meeting the conditions of a promise and receiving the promise is an opportunity for God to show the believer if his faith is genuine or instead if it is a whim or a mere consideration. Notice the following passage.

(Heb 11:13) <u>These all died in faith, not having received the promises</u>, but <u>having seen</u> them afar off, and <u>were persuaded</u> of *them*, and <u>embraced *them*</u>, and confessed that they were strangers and pilgrims on the earth.

Notice the three things in the above passage that are our part that we do in order to receive a promise.

1) See or Recognize the Promise in the Bible (having seen)
2) Believe the Promise and Be Persuaded of the Promise. (were persuaded)
3) Embrace the Promise and Claim the Promise for you Own. (embraced them)

You will also notice in the above verse that the reception of the promise did not occur but that they "died in faith, not having received the promise." On the believer's part, if necessary, you want to die trusting in the promises of God instead of live not trusting the promises of God.

This space of time also gives the believer the chance to take a self-examination and also to see where he has put his faith. Jesus asked this very question in an episode in Luke 8:22-25. Notice the following.

(Luke 8:22) Now it came to pass on a certain day, that he went into a ship with his disciples: and he said unto them, Let us go over unto the other side of the lake. And they launched forth. (Luke 8:23) But as they sailed he fell asleep: and there came down a storm of wind on the lake; and they were filled *with water*, and were in jeopardy. (Luke 8:24) And they came to him, and awoke him, saying, Master, master, we perish. Then he arose, and rebuked the wind and the raging of the water: and they ceased, and there was a calm. (Luke 8:25) And he said unto them, <u>Where is your faith</u>? And they being afraid wondered, saying one to another, What manner of man is this! for he commandeth even the winds and water, and they obey him.

The believer that mis-places his faith should not be surprised by the delay that God puts in his life to receive a promise while God is waiting for the believer to correct the location of his faith back to being in God instead of some other place or in some other thing.

It is safe to say that God never has and never will break any promise that He has made.

Even when the faith of the believer is genuine, God has a right to delay the reception of the promise as He sees fit in order to strengthen the character and faith of the believer. Notice the following passage of scripture.

(Num 23:19) <u>God *is* not a man, that he should lie; neither the son of man, that he should repent: hath he said, and shall he not do *it*? or hath he spoken, and shall he not make it good?</u>

In Chapter 14 in this book, Abraham was brought up for an example of impatience in and episode in a time in his life toward God. This episode reveals what typically every believer will have trouble with concerning the promises of God. It is not <u>the what</u> the believer will receive in the promise as much as it is <u>the when</u> the believer will receive the promise of God. Abraham knew that God promised him a son, but he did not know when and got impatient and jumped ahead of God.

Even though God will never break any promise we must remember God's priority is to conform the believer into the image of Christ. For the God of patience to make the believer into the image of Christ, God knows that the believer must develop a healthy dose of patience.

(Rom 8:29) For whom he did foreknow, <u>he also did predestinate *to be* conformed to the image of his Son</u>, that he might be the firstborn among many brethren.

17

The Endurance of Patience and Patience Brings Endurance

When the Bible speaks of endurance in these passages, it is important to first note what we are expected to endure.

In the verses below God speaks of enduring temptation, the very chastening hand of God, a great fight of afflictions, suffering, time and delays, and the Bible even generally speaks of enduring all things.

When an individual believer endures temptation, it means that he does not yield to temptation but learns from the experience of the temptation and gets away from the lure of the temptation.

(Jas 1:12) <u>Blessed *is* the man that endureth #5278 temptation</u>: for when he is tried, he shall receive the crown of life, which the Lord hath promised to them that love him.

When the believer experiences the chastening hand of God, he does not get angry with God but trusts God and learns from his own sins and takes the punishment with the right attitude and becomes better through it all.

(Heb 12:7) <u>If ye endure #5278 chastening</u>, God dealeth with you as with sons; for what son is he whom the father chasteneth not?

When he is faced with a great fight of afflictions and suffering, he stays alert and learns from each trouble and trial building a stronger and stronger relationship with God through the process.

(Heb 10:32) But call to remembrance the former days, in which, after ye were illuminated, <u>ye endured #5278 a great fight of afflictions</u>;

(2Cor 1:6) And whether we be afflicted, *it is* for your consolation and salvation, which is effectual in the <u>enduring #5281 of the same sufferings</u> which we also suffer: or whether we be comforted, *it is* for your consolation and salvation.

When the believer endures to the end, it is not referring to the salvation of his soul but to the saving of his life. He stays faithful through time and never gives up and his life is victorious and successful all the way to the end. He will be rewarded well in heaven.

(Matt 10:22) And ye shall be hated of all *men* for my name's sake: but <u>he that endureth #5278 to the end shall be saved.</u>

(Matt 24:13) But <u>he that shall endure #5278 unto the end, the same shall be saved</u>.

Mark 13:13) And ye shall be hated of all *men* for my name's sake: but <u>he that shall endure #5278 unto the end, the same shall be saved.</u>

To endure being hated of all men when we are commanded to love all men requires patience. We have to develop as quickly as possible unconditional love that God has and shares instead of trying to operate like the world does with conditional love. The wonderful quality and strength of patience will serve you well in a world filled with hatred. This would be a good time to read the following passage again.

(1Pet 2:20) For what glory *is it*, if, when ye be buffeted for your faults, ye shall take it patiently? but if, <u>when ye do well, and suffer *for it*, ye take it patiently, this *is* acceptable with God.</u>

What we are expected to endure is summarized in the verse below. We are to endure all things.

(1Cor 13:7) Beareth all things, believeth all things, hopeth all things, <u>endureth #5278 all things</u>.

You want to keep the verse below in mind when it comes to enduring all things.

(Phil 4:13) I can do all things through Christ which strengtheneth me.

One of the reasons for the why or what the value is in our patiently enduring is for the elect's sake that will be coming after us. As a believer, remember you are being watched and it is important to set the right example to our lost and dying world. Notice the following passage.

(Matt 5:16) Let your light so shine before men, that they may see your good works, and glorify your Father which is in heaven.

There will be new believers coming after us that we can help pave the way for them instead of making it harder for them. All this is done by patiently enduring.

(2Tim 2:10) Therefore <u>I endure #5278 all things for the elect's sakes</u>, that they may also obtain the salvation which is in Christ Jesus with eternal glory.

The greatest example that exists is the suffering that our Lord Jesus did on the cross to pay for our sins in order to save our souls from Hell.

(Heb 12:2) Looking unto Jesus the author and finisher of *our* faith; who for the joy that was set before him <u>endured #5278 the cross</u>, despising the shame, and is set down at the right hand of the throne of God. (Heb 12:3) For consider him that endured #5278 such contradiction of sinners against himself, lest ye be wearied and faint in your minds.

Allow me to remind you that the verb "endured" in Heb. 12:3 is in the perfect tense. The perfect tense tells us that an act that was once done has everlasting results. This tells us that what Jesus did for us on the cross gives us everlasting life as each of us puts our faith in Christ to be our Savior and Jesus sets an everlasting example for us all.

So, the outcome of the patiently enduring is genuine happiness and the blessing of receiving the wonderful promises of God.

(Jas 5:11) Behold, we count them happy which endure #5278. Ye have heard of the patience #5281 of Job, and have seen the end of the Lord; that the Lord is very pitiful, and of tender mercy.

(Heb 6:15) And so, after he had patiently endured #3114, he obtained the promise.

18

A Comparison of Patience with Procrastination

(Ps 32:9) <u>Be ye not as the horse, *or* as the mule,</u> *which* have no understanding: whose mouth must be held in with bit and bridle, lest they come near unto thee.

The horse is typically known as being impatient. It will be the one that will get more woes and pulling in on the reigns to get them to stop or slow down. This is the model example for the impatient one.

The mule will be the one that is typically stubborn and will get more "git-e-ups" and kicks in the rib to get them to move forward. This is the model example for the procrastinator.

In outward appearance, the one that is patiently waiting on God will look like the one who is actually postponing or procrastinating what God has instructed for him to do.

The patient one will be mistaken for not caring because they are not frantic or overanxious.

Some people who did not have the inside story on many situations that I was involved in as a pastor with the church accused me of procrastination when in truth I was waiting on God to give the guidance and go-ahead or for God to work things out. By the way, God always worked things out just fine.

When Jesus was asleep in a boat during a storm, he was accused of not caring. Notice the passage below.

(Mark 4:37) And there arose a great storm of wind, and the waves beat into the ship, so that it was now full. (Mark 4:38) And he was in the hinder part of the ship, asleep on a pillow: and they awake him, and say unto him, <u>Master, carest thou not that we perish</u>?

Just because the individual is not frantic and is not worried does not mean they do not care.

The procrastinator uses time as a cover-up and a stall for avoiding the obvious engagement of doing. Remember, "not now" to Satan is just as good as a "no." Notice the following passage.

(Prov 3:27) Withhold not good from them to whom it is due, when it is in the power of thine hand to do *it*. (Prov 3:28) Say not unto thy neighbour, Go, and come again, and to morrow I will give; when thou hast it by thee.

Now, notice a comparison of "Can't versus Won't." When Mr. Patient knows what God wants. He will look for God to enable him and make known to him when to proceed and <u>until he gets God's go-ahead he can't proceed</u>. Remember, God is not going to judge the believer in this life by what he can't do. God will judge the believer in this life by what he won't do. Notice the next passage of scripture.

(1Thess 5:24) Faithful *is* he that calleth you, who also will do *it*.

Mr. Procrastinator will know what God wants but will not be seeking from God the enablement needed and the okay from God to proceed. <u>He simply won't</u>. He injects delays and excuses to avoid doing what he knows he should do. Notice the next passage.

(Luke 14:16) Then said he unto him, A certain man made a great supper, and bade many: (Luke 14:17) And sent his servant at supper time to say to them that were bidden, <u>Come; for all things are now ready</u>. (Luke 14:18) And <u>they all with one *consent* began to make excuse</u>. The first said unto him, I have bought a piece of ground, and I must needs go and see it: I pray thee have me excused. (Luke 14:19) And another said, I have bought five yoke of oxen, and I go to prove them: I pray thee have me excused. (Luke 14:20) And another said, I have married a wife, and therefore I cannot come.

It is not that the individuals in the story above could not go, they simply would not go. Allow me to share with you a mathematical equation in the Bible. It is in the following passage.

(1John 5:14) And this is the confidence that we have in him, that, <u>if we ask any thing according to his will, he heareth us:</u>

The mathematical equation goes like this.

If you want it and God wants it, you get it. If God wants it and you do not have it. It is because you do not want it.

There is a definite time to wait on God but when God makes the next move clear and gives you the ability to proceed, the wait is over, and the believer needs to proceed. Remember, <u>Ability plus Availability equals Responsibility</u>.

(Jas 4:17) Therefore <u>to him that knoweth to do good, and doeth *it* not, to him it is sin</u>.

19

Patience while Aging and Patience with those Who are Aging

In the following passage God very beautifully describes growing old and the physical drama that our body will go through as our body progressively starts to fail.

Ecclesiastes 12:1 Remember now thy Creator in the days of thy youth, <u>while the evil days</u> come not, nor the years draw nigh, when thou shalt say, I have no pleasure in them; 2 While the sun, or the light, or the moon, or the stars, be not darkened, nor the clouds return after the rain:

God is reminding us to do what we can for God while we can. Do what you are able to do for God while you are able.

God is also letting us know that our days are seemingly going by faster and faster. The cycle of the sun, moon, stars, sunshine, clouds, and rain will seem to go by quicker and quicker and time will seem to fly by.

God Addresses the Failing Condition of our Hands, Back, Teeth, and our Eyes

3 In the day when the <u>keepers of the house</u> shall tremble, and the <u>strong men</u> shall bow themselves, and the <u>grinders</u> cease because they are few, and <u>those that look out</u> of the windows be darkened,

> *Our "keepers of the house" or our hands will begin to tremble or shake and our "strong men" or back will no longer be able to stand up straight and bear the load that it once did. We will start losing our teeth or "grinders." Our eyes or "those that look out of the windows" will grow dimmer and dimmer requiring more light to see until they go out.*

God addresses the Condition of our Hearing and Sleeplessness

4 And the doors shall be shut in the streets, when <u>the sound of the grinding is low</u>, and <u>he shall rise up at the voice of the bird</u>, and <u>all the daughters of musick shall be brought low;</u>

> *Our hearing will get worse and worse. We will be easily awakened due to our sleeplessness.*

God addresses our Fear of Heights and our Gray and White Hair

5 Also when <u>they shall be afraid of that which is high</u>, and fears shall be in the way, and <u>the almond tree shall flourish</u>, and <u>the grasshopper shall be a burden</u>, and <u>desire shall fail</u>: because <u>man goeth to his long home</u>, and the mourners go about the streets:

> *Note: The fear of heights will get stronger and it is due to the fear of falling and breaking. We will be easily afraid for our physical safety and health. The almond tree shall flourish. The white blossoms of the almond tree are said to be the white hair in old age. Little jobs will become a burden and our personal goals will be more difficult to reach. We will not be able to do what we once wanted to and were able to do in our youth. Then we will finally go to our long home which is heaven. There will be a funeral for our body on earth or "the mourners go about the streets."*

God describes Death and Returning to God

6 Or ever <u>the silver cord be loosed</u>, or <u>the golden bowl be broken</u>, or <u>the pitcher be broken</u> at the fountain, or <u>the wheel broken at the cistern</u>. 7 Then shall <u>the dust return to the earth as it was: and the spirit shall return unto God who gave it.</u>

> *Note: The silver cord being loosed is another way of describing death. Our soul and spirit or loosed and*

separated from our body at death. The golden bowl being broken and the pitcher being broken will no longer contain what they were designed for. The body being broken will no longer contain the soul and spirit at death. The wheel broken at the cistern or well is not able to draw the water of life from the well anymore. The dust is the building material for the body which returns to the ground.

How patient we need to be with ourselves as we get older and older. How patient we need to be with others around us they are growing older and older. God gives us an average and a ball-park figure when our time on earth typically is drawing to a close. Notice the following passage.

(Ps 90:10) The days of our years *are* <u>threescore years and ten; and if by reason of strength *they be* fourscore years, yet *is* their strength labour and sorrow; for it is soon cut off, and we fly away.</u>

Notice the following verses in the Bible where the aging believer cries out to God for help.

(Ps 71:9) <u>Cast me not off in the time of old age; forsake me not when my strength faileth.</u>

(Ps 71:18) Now also <u>when I am old and grayheaded, O God, forsake me not</u>; until I have shewed thy strength unto *this* generation, *and* thy power to every one *that* is to come.

We will get older, but we must know and realize that the promises of God will never expire or get old. God has promised he will never leave us nor forsake us. Notice the following.

(Ps 37:25) <u>I have been young, and *now* am old; yet have I not seen the righteous forsaken,</u> nor his seed begging bread.

(Heb 13:5) Let your conversation be without covetousness; and be content with such things as ye have: for he hath said, <u>I will never leave thee, nor forsake thee.</u>

There is the tendency to lose respect for the elderly when they get up in years because they become more and more limited on what they are able to do. We even have the cruel tendency to lose respect for our own parents thinking that they are a burden to us and society. Notice the following passage.

(Prov 23:22) Hearken unto thy father that begat thee, and <u>despise not thy mother when she is old.</u>

There is the feeling that as we get older that we will lose more and more of our usefulness and think that our value is also decreasing. We as believers must go to church as much as we are able to, even as we get older and older. Notice the following passage.

(Ps 92:13) Those that be planted in the house of the LORD shall flourish in the courts of our God. (Ps 92:14)

<u>They shall still bring forth fruit in old age</u>; they shall be fat and flourishing;

> *No matter how old we get we must always as believers strive to do right and live right and keep the right attitude. Notice the following.*

(Prov 16:31) <u>The hoary head *is* a crown of glory, *if* it be found in the way of righteousness.</u>

(Prov 20:29) The glory of young men *is* their strength: and <u>the beauty of old men *is* the gray head.</u>

> *We already know as we age our strength will become less and less. We must patiently accept the fact that there will be more and more things that we will not be able to do. I do remember that at one time in my life I use to be able to run. Now, I am thrilled that I am still so far able to walk.*

> *We become more and more dependent on outside help and crutches. We must patiently adjust with the tools available to assist us in whatever task we are trying to do. I have seen a lot of sorrow in the life of the one that has been told that they are no longer able to drive a vehicle due to their age.*

> *We must do whatever we can to keep our minds sharp. I have been able to witness many individuals who were great in age and their minds were still extremely sharp.*

Allow me to inject a personal note concerning our memory as we age. I must confess that the one thing I fear the most as I age is memory loss. I believe I fear Alzheimer's disease more than getting cancer. Remember that whatever befall us, Jesus doeth all things well and Jesus will never forsake us.

Be aware that we sometimes give credit to memory failure when we multitask and are thinking of other things while doing some things and do not remember what we did. It is not that we do not remember, it is that we had our minds elsewhere and what we were doing was not on our mind from the beginning. Your mind cannot forget what has never been put into your mind.

As long as you can, as a believer, you must read your Bible regularly and use your mind wisely as much as you possibly can.

It is true that as we get older, we will forget a lot of things and maybe we will forget who we are. It is true that it is possible for the elderly to forget their own children and their own grandchildren and even their own mate. However, <u>we must never forget who the loved ones are that are losing their memories</u>.

(Prov 17:6) Children's children *are* the crown of old men; and the glory of children *are* their fathers.

Remember the most powerful thing any believer can do is pray. To ask God for help for someone else or for yourself is the most powerful thing you can do because nothing is more powerful than God and when God moves to help, there is nothing that can stop Him. Some of the most powerful prayer warriors are believers that have gotten well up in age.

If you can think, you can pray. Please consider this. Because you can think, you can pray right up to the last day of your life on earth. This should stop Satan or anyone else from trying to convince you that you are useless. There is a passage of scripture that tells us when the soul and spirit leave the body and they pass on in death. Notice the following.

(Ps 146:1) Praise ye the LORD. Praise the LORD, O my soul. (Ps 146:2) <u>While I live will I praise the LORD</u>: I will sing praises unto my God <u>while I have any being</u>. (Ps 146:3) Put not your trust in princes, *nor* in the son of man, in whom *there is* no help. (Ps 146:4) <u>His breath goeth forth, he returneth to his earth</u>; <u>in that very day his thoughts perish.</u>

Physically, your thoughts perish the moment you die. In other words when a person's brain activity stops, their soul has left their body. As long as you are thinking you can be praying for someone. This means you are never useless.

One of the horrible things that has been produced due to the impatience of humanity is what the world calls, "Euthanasia." What can humanity be thinking?

Are we so impatient that we are ready to step in and take someone's life due to aging because we think that they are no longer good for society and they are useless? Do finances get involved thinking that it would be easier and cheaper to take their life than to do whatever it takes to help them live and live in comfort? Are we ready to take their life upon request of the one aging or upon a vote of family members or an okay by the physicians involved?

Remember if the elderly has not trusted Christ as their Savior, Hell is waiting for them. So, the family and friends would be wise to give out the plan of salvation verbally as much as possible to the elderly while the elderly is alive. Be aware that the last physical sense of the five senses typically to go when dying is the hearing.

One of the events that is precious in life is to be present and witness when a loved one that is saved dies. In spite of pain and drugs, the dying testimony of a believer to the friends and family members is priceless especially if they share their dying experience verbally while they are leaving for heaven.

(Ps 90:10) The days of our years *are* threescore years and ten; and if by reason of strength *they be* fourscore years, <u>yet *is* their strength labour and sorrow</u>; for it is soon cut off, and <u>we fly away</u>.

20

Summary Comments about "Patience"

Allow me to give one last glimpse of the 7 Greek words on patience and their word study sentences. Notice again the set of English synonyms and short phrase definitions for patience coming from these Greek words as used in the King James Bible.

G420 (1x)(patient) 2 Tim 2:24

G1933 (5x)(gentle-3; moderation; patient)

G3114 (10x)(be patient-3; have patience-2; have long patience; bear

long; suffer long; be longsuffering; patiently endure)

G3115 (14x)(longsuffering-12; patience-2)

G3116 (1x)(patiently) Acts 26:3

G5278 (17x)(endure-11; take patiently-2; tarry behind; abide; patient; suffer)

G5281 (32x)(patient continuance; enduring; patience-29; patient waiting)

To be patient is a command to us from God. God expects us to be patient toward all men and remember that all includes ourselves as well. We must be patient in everything.

God tells us to be patient toward the second coming of Christ and the key to this is to occupy until Jesus comes back. Staying busy for God helps with also not giving up or being impatient while looking for Jesus to come back.

(Luke 19:13) And he called his ten servants, and delivered them ten pounds, and said unto them, <u>Occupy till I come</u>.

When tribulation comes our way, we need to allow patience to work and develop to stop us from panicking when we are taken out of our comfort zone. Remember, trials and tribulations are always a time of learning. We must prepare ourselves to take notes and learn as much as possible through the trials that come our way. If we are alert, during the trials we can learn much more about ourselves and others and God. It is when we are out of our comfort zone that we will learn much more about ourselves, good and bad.

We must be patient with God's chastisement on us because it helps us to take the spiritual spanking to heart and not to pass the blame of our sin on others. We must remember that God is making us more like Jesus and intends on fulfilling the promise. Notice the following passage.

(Rom 8:29) For whom he did foreknow, <u>he also did predestinate *to be* conformed to the image of his Son,</u> that he might be the firstborn among many brethren.

We should not be surprised that patience is a required and major part of the ministry of the preacher that pastors a church or for the preacher that preaches God's Word but does not pastor. God requires patience for every part of the ministry.

God commends three of the seven churches mentioned in the Book of Revelation for their patience.

We are commanded by God to be patient in running the race of service for God. We are to be patient in order to bear fruit and patient in listening and even patient in receiving the promises of God.

Patience gives us the opportunity to wait on God and follow His guidance each step of the way in our lives.

(Ps 37:23) <u>The steps of a *good* man are ordered by the LORD</u>: and he delighteth in his way.

Gerald McDaniel

Patience helps us to trust in the providential hand of God to work in our lives as God sees fit.

Patience stops the believer from jumping to conclusions and from guessing or speculating or jumping ahead of God.

(Rom 14:23) And he that doubteth is damned if he eat, because *he eateth* not of faith: for whatsoever *is* not of faith is sin.

Patience allows us to humble ourselves before God and to shun the pride in our lives that would draw us to do our own will instead of God's will.

(Luke 22:42) Saying, Father, if thou be willing, remove this cup from me: nevertheless not my will, but thine, be done.

God has set the example for every believer with His patience toward vengeance and toward people getting saved and toward the believers with His guiding and chastening hand. We should not be surprised that God is called "The God of Patience."

(Rom 15:5) Now the God of patience and consolation grant you to be likeminded one toward another according to Christ Jesus:

In closing allow me to remind the reader about the statement that God says about patience and the believer's soul.

(Luke 21:19) In your patience possess ye your souls.

Printed in the United States
By Bookmasters